A
REVELATION
OF THE CROSS

by

Nancy L. Eskijian

A Revelation of the Cross
by Nancy L. Eskijian

Signalman Publishing
www.signalmanpublishing.com
email: info@signalmanpublishing.com
Kissimmee, Florida

Cover design by Rob Cheney

All Scripture quotes are from the King James Bible unless otherwise noted.

Scripture taken from The Message. Copyright© 1993, 1994, 1995, 1996, 2000, 2001, 2002. Used by permission of NavPress Publishing Group.
Scripture taken from the New King James Version. Copyright © 1982 by Thomas Nelson, Inc. Used by permission. All rights reserved.
Scripture quotations marked (NLT) are taken from the Holy Bible, New Living Translation, copyright © 1996, 2004, 2007 by Tyndale House Foundation. Used by permission of Tyndale House Publishers, Inc., Carol Stream, Illinois 60188. All rights reserved.

ISBN: 978-1-940145-61-7 (paperback)
      978-1-940145-62-4 (ebook)

Library of Congress Control Number: 2016945239
2017 Update.

Printed in the United States of America

SIGNALMAN
PUBLISHING

Dedicated to Jesus Christ

"Unto him that loved us, and washed us from our sins in his own blood…" Revelation 1:5

CONTENTS

PART I: Summation of the Cross

PART II: A Revelation of the Cross

PART III: The Destination of the Cross

Foreword

A Revelation of the Cross is a journey into the heart of God and His journey into our hearts. The cross is the only way God could reach us, piercing our innermost being by a divine death and resurrection. The cross is intended to be a sword that cuts deep into the heart of the earth with love, penetrating the pain of a planet, the curses on the planet, and the sin of the planet. The cross is a God type of love: Big, massive, bold, lavish, like creation—just in the reverse—supernatural suffering, death and sorrow, for supernatural sin and its consequences and penalties. <u>This book</u> is not about human stories. It is drilling down to the mother lode of the love and blood of Jesus Christ. <u>This book</u> is designed to start a fire of passion in your heart and mark you exclusively for God. **<u>This book</u>** *is a divine love story that has no end, and is intended to ruin you for anything but God. This book is dedicated "Unto him that loved us, and washed us from our sins in his own blood,..." Revelation 1:5*

Part I

Summation of the Cross

CHAPTER ONE

In the Beginning, If I Be Lifted Up
The Urgency of the Cross

And as Moses lifted up the serpent in the wilderness, even so must the Son of man be lifted up. That whosoever believeth in Him should not perish, but have eternal life. For God so loved the world that He gave His only begotten Son, that whosoever believeth in Him should not perish be have everlasting life. John 3:14-16.

And I, if I be lifted up from the earth, will draw all men unto Me. John 12:32

In His final days, Jesus said, "If I be lifted up I will draw all men unto Me." Suddenly, a Passover later, He was hung, bloody and battered, between heaven and earth for the whole world to see. Today in the final moments of this age, the power of the cross must be preached and released, so multitudes can be reached for the Savior. It is and always has been the Father's urgent plan. Only the cross completely contrasts God's ways, our ways, the world's ways, and the devil's ways. Only through the cross is the mystery of the heart of God, and the secrets of our hearts, completely revealed. The cross is a place of crisis, truth, love and reconciliation. There a loving God and willing men and women may express love to each other and be connected once again because the Son of God paves the way by His own humility and humiliation.

Even though Satan thought he owned the situation, he is excluded, for the love released at the cross totally breaks his power and dominion. The enemy of God was God's tool for mercy. Satan the god of this world thought he had won, but his winning was his losing, and our losing our lives in and to Christ becomes our winning. It is the divine pattern. Divine love is first of all inclusive, but then exclusive. It does not include the enemy.

The cross is both completely public, as the Lord broadcasts His matchless love for all time; and totally private, as we confess our unfaithfulness to Him. Jesus bears our shame and His blood covers us. The preaching of the cross is foolishness to the world, but it is the divine, unequaled magnet of love.

The cross is re-creation's story. It is the heart of God exposed—the passionate pouring out of His love to get us back. The cross is the journey to the center of God's heart to restore us and the planet. At the cross "sons of men" die, stale kingdoms overthrown, and unnatural orders based in sin reversed, so that new men and women may be born again and made alive in Jesus Christ the Risen King.

The world without the Savior is crying and dying. Multitudes stand in the waiting rooms of time or eternity; if they do not hear of His love and experience the cross, they will experience endless time instead of everlasting life. One day, the day of grace will end and the final judgments begin. One day the door of love will close.

Already the birth pangs of a new planet are breaking on the shores of this earth. In the beginning God **so loved** His first **son,** Adam, that He **gave** him the **world**. At the cross God **so loved** the **world** that He **gave** His only begotten **Son,** Jesus, the Second Adam, to save the world. Passion created this world, compassion has saved it. Adam despised his inheritance and the free gift of God's love. The cross is God's final message of salvation: Do not reject His love a second time. Today we must tell them of the cross and compel them to come in. The cross is the new start for the human race that we may be prepared for a new heaven and a new earth in a harvest of grace: His blood for ours.

At the cross
God destroyed the human race
Not by fire or flood,
Judgment's blood
Was mixed with grace.

CHAPTER TWO

The Great Reversal

The cross is ground zero. It was the day the love of God leveled the earth. It was a day things got so bad that they got good. There the great reversal began, until the moment Jesus cried, "It is finished" and the Son of God died.

At the cross, there was an earthquake and a heaven-quake, then tidal waves of love flattened earthly kingdoms, and rivers of life flowed with the blood of mercy, not judgment, as His blood touched the ground, the Beloved, humble Lover.

AT THE CROSS:

The first become last and the last become first.

The empty become full and the full become empty.

The righteous become sinners and the sinners become righteous.

The religious are rebellious and the sinners are invited.

The rich are wretched, poor, blind, miserable, and naked, and the poor are made rich.

A crucified thief is paradise's guest of honor, and the first convert. His loss becomes his gain. The emptiness of his life and his judgment are miraculously rearranged by divine timing as he exchanges eternal addresses with the Son of God. "Remember me when you come into your kingdom," he says—and that day he was with Jesus in paradise. Luke 23:43.

The Roman executioner who splintered His hands with nails

becomes the second convert. "Truly this was the Son of God," he says. He is stunned, horrified, overcome by the ecstasy of divine love, converted by the shame of his crime and the divine gift offered so freely, flattened by divine reality.

Executed and executioner are saved at the foot of the cross.

The proud are brought low by His humility and the lowly are lifted up. Earth can no longer pretend it is heaven. Heaven is heaven.

His stripped body becomes our covering for sin.

Death is reversed to life.

The worst day in the history of the world, the most despicable evil day, where man displayed his sinfulness, and Satan poured out his hatred, **is reversed to the most glorious day, WHERE GOD'S LOVE WAS SHED.**

Hell is reversed and heaven touched earth. And we could have a new birth.

At the cross the anointing of heaven is released on earth, and the blood of Jesus abolishes the curse.

At the cross, our natural killing instinct is used by God Himself to become the method of our salvation, and the final, truest mirror into human hearts.

The power of all earthly and demonic kingdoms is shaken and broken, all by the immense outpouring of God's love through the blood of Jesus, as they attempted to break God's power.

I John 4:9 makes this profound statement: *⁹God showed how much he loved us by sending his only Son into the world so that we might have eternal life through him. ¹⁰This is real love. It is not that we loved God, but that he loved us and sent his Son as a sacrifice to take away our sins.* In this was the measure of God's love shown— not in creation—but God's release of his Son into the wilderness of the world to be the Lamb slain from the foundation of the world. The measure of His love was the treasure of His Son.

Those overcome by sin, the world, and the devil become overcomers.

The weak conquered by every virus of sin and weakness of the flesh become more than conquerors.

Sons of men become sons of God. Old creation becomes a new creation. <u>Everything ends and everything begins at the cross.</u>

Our flaws are ended and reversed into new beginnings--that we might become overcomers; that we might become more than conquerors; that we might become sons and daughters of God; that we might become new creations; **that we might become, and become and become for eternity**, instead of be damned.

A crown of thorns becomes a crown of glory. And disciples are born each day hungering for the divine. They treasure the One who wore the crown of thorns beyond life itself.

The marring of His face becomes the treasure of His beauty. At the cross, His face was so marred that no one could recognize Him, the prophet Isaiah wrote, <u>BUT LOVE HAD A FACE THAT DAY.</u> He emptied Himself and took all our faces and the <u>blankness of our lost identities</u>—God allowed Him to be unrecognizable. He paid the penalty, and took the judgment. He took the blank face of the human race and hung there for us in disgrace.

Condemned prisoners are freed and redeemed.

The scene of an old, old, story becomes the only place in a modern, technical, sophisticated, selfish world where we can find new refreshing truth. **In the end there is no place in this universe to go but the cross to find true life and love. You can't find God anywhere else than the cross, and you can't know Him elsewhere except by the cross. You can't find yourself anywhere but at the cross.** And you can't know others except through the cross. You can't find yourself until you lose yourself. All our missing pieces cannot be restored on earth, but only by heaven, through the cross.

The cross is a place where we can reclaim our lost identity by recognizing our "lostness."

All true roads lead to the cross of Jesus Christ, and his divine Person and love and the heavenly city. The dusty sweat and blood stained road to the cross is the road to glory, the road to heaven.

The tree of death is the tree of life.

It is the Mount of Transfiguration for the disfigured soul.

War in our hearts becomes the path of peace on earth. There is no peace except by the blood of the cross, peace with heaven and peace on earth and peace inside.

At the cross, the Trinity was divided, so we could be put back together again. The Father turned away from His Son, and the Holy Spirit could not stay where there was sin, and the Son went to the grave and Hades. Had Jesus failed, the Godhead would have been split for eternity, but Jesus didn't fail because God is love, Jesus is God, and love never fails.

At the cross, where force was released in perverted display, we must lay our weapons down. All scores in heaven, on earth and in hearts are settled. In this way, His kingdom will come and His will be done.

Innocent and guilty meet at the cross, the innocent for healing, the guilty for forgiveness, and both for restoration.

Because of the cross, the angel of death can be stopped streets of our cities as it travels to bring destruction. Instead angels come with mercy.

A sad day becomes a glad day. The cross joins families across the ages in eternal reunion.

Those who were destined to become eternally separated from Him, become eternally married to Him.

The cross is evidence of God's unstoppable love. The resurrection is evidence of God's unstoppable power.

The shameful act that appeared to leave no room for forgiveness, brings forgiveness.

The cross is the one sliver on earth that connects heaven and earth eternally, where sins can be erased and we can experience His grace.

The sun which hid its face in shame will later shine with the grace of God on a new order of creation through the Son of God.

The despised Son of God becomes the greatest role model on

earth, the Leader of the Universe, who saved His people from their sins at the cross.

Every good thing we possess, know, and are, stems from the awful stripping of the cross.

God should have punished the world because of the cross, but He loved the world by it instead.

He should have destroyed the planet because of its sinfulness, but instead He gave us the cross. The world would explode without the cross. The cross is the stabilizing core of this earth holding back the judgments and curses that long ago would have demolished us.

The church is built on the apostles and prophets, the universe is founded on the Living Word Jesus, but blood of the cross holds the world together. The purpose of the church is to bring the world and struggling believers over the "It is Finished" line of the cross.

Kings and leaders will bow to the King of the cross, the altar of execution.

The cross is the crossroads of every life--you will either leave your burdens down, decide to forgive and love, believe in Jesus Christ and do it His way, or will you go your own way into outer darkness.

There is no middle ground at the cross; it is ground zero for the planet. There are no preferences, no favorites. It cuts across every tribe, nation, race, and people. There is no special treatment at the cross, no special categories, no special people, no special sin, and no special favors.

There is no competition with the cross.

There is no compromise at the cross.

There is no communion without the cross

There is no Christ without the cross.

There are no lies at the cross.

There is no ultimate love without the cross.

There is no ultimate peace without the cross.

There is no ultimate truth without the cross.

There is no salvation without the cross.

There is no God without the cross.

The cross is for those who truly want answers. It is for those who want to know God. The cross is not our enemy, it is our destiny.

The cross the great equalizer, it pulls down every high thing, every human distinction, and lifts up every low thing. It is a blast of global nuclear proportions that sifts the hearts of every person into either particles of glory or chaff, sifting the real and counterfeit.

By the cross we learn that God is fair, His balances are always just and right, and He has made a way for us to measure up, by ending us and beginning Him.

Earth may be rearranged, but never changed, except by the cross.

His love re-forms us, transforms us, and conforms us to His image, and takes us out of what is deformed and accelerates what is unformed in us.

The crucifixion is the day the earth stood still. Time stopped and the sun hid its face for three hours of agony and glory.

The cross is the door of God's anointing to earth that we may be released to heaven.

At the cross we see the power in the death of God and the power in the life of God.

The Father didn't answer the Son's prayer at the Garden of Gethsemane to be released from the cup of suffering He would experience at the cross, but He answered ours. While God does not always provide a rescue, He does promise a resurrection.

By the cross the crooked is made straight, and the rough places plain.

The cross is the great separator. It separates today—those who will humble themselves and those who remain proud, those who ask forgiveness, and those who see no need of forgiveness, those who forgive and those who won't, those who fall on the Rock, Jesus, and those who become like a rock, those who choose to love and those who choose to hate, people who hold on and people who let go, those who want to be happy, and those who want to be holy and whole, those who want to be right, and those who want to be righteous.

Then it separates some more. It separates the sinner from sin, sickness from the sick, demons from the demonized, self from the self, the soul from the spirit, foolishness from the fool, generational patterns from the vulnerable, blindness from the blind, death from the dead, and the judged from the forgiven.

The cross, a despised symbol for losers to the world, a crutch and joke, ***IS OUR SECOND CHANCE, OUR LAST CHANCE, OUR BEST CHANCE, OUR ONLY CHANCE.*** Our only mistake will be not to take it far enough, deep enough, wide enough.

We will either be conquered by the love of the cross or judged by it. The cross will either break the shell of hell around us, or we will be entrapped by hell eternally.

Most people despise the cross, yet many still slip in one by one through the gate of the cross to be saved, healed, set free. It is an instrument of death where we can begin life again.

Life becomes un-crowded at the cross. It is the straight and narrow gate and we wonder where all the friends and loved ones are. At the cross He takes us in one by one. Every encounter at the cross is a personal moment. God the Father, God the Son, God the Spirit, the Holy One, you and me and the greater One, triangle of endless love. It is us and Him, no excuses, no favors, no hiding. He does not shame us at the cross, or blame us at the cross, He took that. He forgives, releases and heals us at the cross. The cross reduces and diffuses all human excuses.

The cross will both break and/or make us, every day of our lives.

The cross is the wrecking ball of the world.

The winner touches the cross, the winner takes all through the cross, the winner possesses all power in heaven and earth through the cross.

It is the sword of the Lord to conquer our hearts.

At the cross, Jesus miraculously turns shame into glory, death into life, foolishness into wisdom, as miraculously as He turned water into wine, and sickness into health. Jesus reverses everything at the cross, the stains of His blood wiped out the stains of all blood shed on a rebellious, blind, hard, wicked, beloved planet from the foundation of the world.

At the cross, all the blood of the Son was poured to the ground, as a drink offering, the cup of suffering, so that we could experience, the cup of communion, the cup of life, and the outpouring of the Holy Spirit.

The fact that Jesus Christ took all the filth and degradation of this planet on Himself proves there is a God, that Jesus Christ is the Son of God, that God loves Earth, and that He created it for His glory. The Father did this through the hands of His Son, by the power of the Holy Spirit, first in initial creation, and then through the hands of His Son, through the Eternal Spirit, as they touched wood and became broken clay on the day of His death in our re-creation.

The glory of the cross!

CHAPTER THREE

The Reason for the Cross

The cross of Jesus Christ is the most important event in the history of the world. All life on this planet centers around the cross, whether all life on the planet knows it or not. With the cross comes the resurrection. Unstoppable love and unstoppable power are the message of the cross and the resurrection—God compressed in all time and eternity into a great compression. We see all the eternal and human attributes of God for now and ever. Through the cross we have the opportunity to end an old, sinful life, and enter into new life, through the resurrection.

The cross and resurrection are what makes us the people of God and sets us apart. It is about holiness. Jesus totally immersed Himself in our experience, our suffering and separation from God, and our ordinary lives. The cross is God's throne of grace on earth, for the Lord goes low, so we can go high, and become holy instead of profane.

At the cross, Jesus takes away our fantasies and gives us reality. He takes away our pride so we can become great in Him. He became one of us, so we could become like Him. He gave us a love more real than any other love, a love that passes through life and death. The cross is as important today as it was 2000 years ago. People still yearn for truth somewhere. People still yearn for love, to know and be known. He is full of grace and truth. People crave to understand their internal opposition to life and get out of the death trap they are in. They crave to be understood, and the Lord does all of this because He has travelled our path, embraced flesh and blood, experienced our wounds, known our dreams and nightmares, experienced our traumas, went through our death and made the way for our resurrection. There He utterly turns us inside out and ruins us to the world. There He displayed Himself in humiliation so we can present to Him our insanity, rebellion, pain, contradictions and more in humility at the cross.

The cross is a place of real and eternal hope and change, because Christ reaches into the depths of our souls through His blood and cleanses us and restores us, and makes us whole. Die there and live. Reject the cross and die. Humble yourself there, and be raised up. Stay proud and be destroyed. Admit your sins and wickedness, give away shame and guilt, leave the sorrows, every day, leave the sickness and death, and rise up like the new people that God originally intended us to be. He gives us hope because we can change to be like Him--holy. Holy brings healed. Holy opens the door for happy. God so loved us, but His love is transformational, because it is living, and it is purposeful, making possible heaven's will on earth.

The pattern of the cross is the theme of the Bible. It is the pattern of living and loving from a living and loving God who created a world that became corrupted and destroyed by sin. We carry that sin nature in the blood, but by the blood of Jesus that sin nature can be interrupted. It takes the blood. The intervention is in the blood. It is the intervention of blood spilled for blood spilled, speaking greater things than the blood of Abel. God's holy blood has power to overthrow the works of the enemy. We know this because:

> [11]For the life of the flesh *is* in the blood, and I have given it to you upon the altar to make atonement for your souls; for it *is* the blood *that* makes atonement for the soul. Leviticus 17:11 (NKJV).

> Hebrews 12:24 (NKJV): [24]to Jesus the Mediator of the new covenant, and to the blood of sprinkling that speaks better things than *that of* Abel. Blood on earth and blood in heaven. Hebrews 12:24 (NKJV).

[28]For this is My blood of the new covenant, which is shed for many for the remission of sins. Matthew 26:28 (NKJV).

To Him who loved us and washed us from our sins in His own blood. Revelation 1:5.

Blood was first shed after Adam and Eve first sinned in the Garden of Eden. God killed animals and clothed Adam and Eve. And so the pattern continued, as sacrifices were made of innocent animals, to cover sins with the blood of sacrifice, the innocent for the guilty. But in these last days, once and for all the blood has been shed, to erase our sins, and the cross stands as a new start for our lives, where we die and He lives. God exchanges all that He is for all that we are. It is a royal and divine transaction. Like the pearl of great price, we give all that we are to obtain the depth and riches of the cross.

At the cross was the ultimate exchange. Blood for blood, death for death, life for life, joy for sorrow, thorns for a crown—it could not be more serious and complete, the death of God was necessary to absorb the death of man, for the life of man was created in the image of God and is released and redeemed in the cross.

Jesus was a prisoner of the cross. He was born for the cross, He lived for the cross, and He died on the cross. He could not escape the cross without losing Who He was, and who we are. We cannot escape the cross without losing who we are either. His purpose was the cross, His direction was the cross, He never escaped the cross. He is forever identified with the cross because of the eternal exchange that would happen at the cross. He was liberated from this prison at the resurrection. Jesus could not escape the destiny of the cross without going to the cross, and He could not purchase the destiny of the cross for us, without the cross. There was a prisoner exchange at the cross, His life for ours.

The cross was the only way a loving God could change the inner man. But with that change is eternal hope, not a hope that can be taken away, but one that is part of our life, our spiritual DNA. He intended us to be like Him—spiritual men and women with eternal life in us. He said, be ye holy for I am holy.

The cross defines truth, the cross defines love, the cross defines God, and the cross defines us. Only when the cross pierces our hearts can we surrender to God, and we can only surrender to God when the cross pierces our hearts. There are times when the cross can pierce our flesh or our minds or our feet or hands, but it is only when the cross pierces our hearts that we can become new and the covenant is made.

Jesus travelled on a journey from heaven to earth to hell and then back to earth and then heaven. It was a treacherous journey. The Father knew the outcome—but it still took faith to release His Son. Jesus had to walk by faith. He wasn't on earth to get wealth, raise a family, be famous, or live a good life. Jesus experienced the opposite of these things, He became poor, so we could become rich, He did not have a natural family, so He could have a spiritual one, He was despised and rejected, famous only for humiliation, and as for a good life, He had nowhere to lay His head. Someday, He will embrace the earth as His own when He comes to rule and reign—but not then. Then was the time to purchase us through the blood. He came to us to demonstrate Who God is, and to die and be raised, so that a whole new human race could come up. Jesus came to earth for the cross and the resurrection, and to demonstrate Who God is.

Jesus could have failed. He had choices too. His choices were not easy, He sweat drops of blood. Had He failed, the world and the universe would have collapsed, because the Second Person of the Godhood would no longer exist to uphold it all by the word of His power, and the Triune God would have been separated. Hebrews 1:3. But, as I said, He didn't fail, because love never fails and God is love and Jesus is God.

People loved Him, they hated Him, mocked Him, praised Him, spit on Him, and bathed His feet in perfume and dried them with hair. They nailed His feet to a cross. They embraced Him with their arms and served Him with their hands. But then they hit Him with their hands and clubs and whips and nails and spears. They gave to Him, they stole from Him. They wanted Him dead, they wanted Him saved. They worshipped Him, they scorned Him. They ignored Him, they adored Him. He brought out the extremes of love and sin. The cross forces truth.

Doesn't that show the extremes of the human condition? No matter what, and no matter where we are on that extreme, God so loved. He loved the traitors and betrayers. He loves those who oppose themselves, He loves those who are good and those who are bad. He just loves. And His love is bigger than good and bad. It just is, and takes us back to a time before we were contaminated with the knowledge of good and evil. He is good, and His love endures. He sees into our extreme souls, and our radical opposition to Him and life. He swallows our death because His death is so big on the cross that death is swallowed up in victory, and it shows us that God is bigger than death in the resurrection. He is all life, all the time, all abundant, all resurrection, all supernatural, and all eternal, all the time. There is nothing we experience or are, that cannot be changed at the cross. Put your faith in the God of the cross.

Jesus knew the danger we faced as sinners and came to save sinners—not just keep us from hell. He came to save sinners. When you save sinners you have a relationship.

He cuts it all away at the cross. Makes us all clean and fresh by His blood. He is worthy of all praise and honor. God brings forth a new creation through the cross. God the Creator becomes one with God the Savior.

When John the Baptist saw Jesus he said, Behold the Lamb of God which takes away the sin of the world. Jesus is called the Lamb slain from the foundation of the world. It is His highest title—the sacrifice. He exposed the love of God for everyone to see. People can see creation and wonder, but people marvel and weep at the love of God at the cross.

Jesus Christ died for sinners because sin causes separation from God, self and others, and sin is a destroyer of love and God cannot bear that separation. I John 4:9 states:

> [9]God showed how much he loved us by sending his only Son into the world so that we might have eternal life through him. [10]This is real love. It is not that we loved God, but that he loved us and sent his Son as a sacrifice to take away our sins.

The cross is the scene of the old, old, story:

> [18]I know very well how foolish the message of the cross sounds to those who are on the road to destruction. But we who are being saved recognize this message as the very power of God. [19]As the Scriptures say, "I will destroy human wisdom and discard their most brilliant ideas." [20]So where does this leave the philosophers, the scholars, and the world's brilliant debaters? God has made them all look foolish and has shown their wisdom to be useless nonsense. 1 Corinthians 1:18 - 20 (NLT).

> [18]For the preaching of the cross is to them that perish foolishness; but unto us which are saved it is the power of God. [19]For it is written, I will destroy the wisdom of the wise, and will bring to nothing the understanding of the prudent. 1 Corinthians 1:18 - 19.

There is no competition with the cross.

The cross is foolish to the world. It is for weaklings. It is for people who need to believe in God. It is foolish to think of God taking our sins. Sin doesn't exist. It is foolish to those who perish, but to us who are saved it is the power of God. It is not for strong men or people who are powerful in themselves. That foolishness is the preaching of the cross. But it shows the power of God.

The cross destroys all the wisdom of the wise. God becomes weak, taking all our weakness so we might be strong. God knows we are weak and broken. Jesus Christ loves and bleeds, and don't we all want a God that loves us and bleeds for us. Aren't we tired of serving people who don't give, and ideas that are destructive? Don't we want flesh and blood love? If God doesn't love us, there is no point in being on this planet. But He does love us and He proved it on the cross.

The missing pieces of our lives cannot be restored on earth, but only by heaven, through the cross. The cross is a place where we can reclaim our lost identity by recognizing our "lostness", and coming back home to the Father.

All roads lead to the cross of Jesus Christ. Through the cross we learn that nothing can separate us from the love of God. He didn't leave us. He should have separated Himself from us forever for our sinfulness, but instead He joined Himself to us forever through the cross.

> [31]What can we say about such wonderful things as these? If God is for us, who can ever be against us? [32]Since God did not spare even his own Son but gave him up for us all, won't God, who gave us Christ, also give us everything else? Romans 8:31 - 32 (NLT).

> [35]Can anything ever separate us from Christ's love? Does it mean he no longer loves us if we have trouble or calamity, or are persecuted, or are hungry or cold or in danger or threatened with death? [37]No, despite all these things, overwhelming victory is ours through Christ, who loved us. Romans 8:35 - 37 (NLT).

He suffered because He wanted our love, and because He loved us. He didn't give up on you or me. He paid the price for our souls with His blood. He took the form of a servant. He washed our feet. He died our death, He lived our lives, He breathed our breath, He ate our bread and gave us the Bread of Life.

He carried our grief and sorrows. He labored to birth us. He married us and covered us with His robes of righteousness. He took us into His family, as orphans and strangers. He introduces us to ourselves our true identities that we lost through our weakness and sin and the sins and weakness of others. He builds us a new foundation in our lives. He provides for us, He guides us. He heals us and seals us. He doesn't care what we look like, where we came from, or what we have done, as long as we come to Him.

He says, come home, all is forgiven. He says, you want a real new deal, come unto me all you who labor and are heavy laden and I will give you rest. I will enter into your labors and you will enter into My rest without being degraded and treated as something less than. When human beings use us we feel dirty, but when God uses us we feel clean.

God did come through, and because of that, we are going to come through too. There will be a harvest and although weeping may endure for a night, joy comes in the morning.

CHAPTER FOUR

An Account of the Cross

All the gospels give an account of the crucifixion of Jesus. The Lord wants to make sure that we know this story. The crucifixion is called the passion of Jesus Christ and passion it was. No greater love exists than this-that a man lay down his life for his friends.

Mark 15 (NLT) provides an account of the trial of Jesus, so I am going to start there with the words of Pontius Pilate, the Roman governor who judged Jesus. Pilate is a typical politician: *12 "But if I release Barabbas," Pilate asked them, "what should I do with this man you call the King of the Jews?"*

Pilate the Roman governor is having an issue as to which prisoner to release. Three times he has said, he found no fault in Jesus, but what do you do with an angry mob? Another prisoner by the name of Barabbas is sentenced to death too, but the crowd demanded the death of Jesus. Better to calm down an angry mob than allow one man to live.

> ¹³They shouted back, "Crucify him!" ¹⁴"Why?" Pilate demanded. "What crime has he committed?" But the crowd only roared the louder—"Crucify him!" ¹⁵So Pilate, <u>anxious to please the crowd,</u> released Barabbas to them. He ordered Jesus flogged with a lead-tipped whip, then turned him over to the Roman soldiers to crucify him.

It wasn't that Pilate didn't know who was guilty and who was innocent, he just didn't have the power to act on what was right. The bottom line is that our fallen nature doesn't give us the power to act on what is right. Only through Jesus can we get our power to choose again. The divine irony is that through the cross to which Pilate condemned Jesus by his indecision and weakness, we obtain the power to choose again. Pilate was close to Jesus on that day of judgment—perhaps he was just a few feet away, but He didn't know Jesus. In the end, instead of Jesus being judged that day, Pilate would be judged. The weary, cynical, compromising governor would have his fate sealed that day.

> [16]The soldiers took him into their headquarters and called out the entire battalion. [17]They dressed him in a purple robe and made a crown of long, sharp thorns and put it on his head. [18]Then they saluted, yelling, "Hail! King of the Jews!" [19]And they beat him on the head with a stick, spit on him, and dropped to their knees in mock worship. [20]When they were finally tired of mocking him, they took off the purple robe and put his own clothes on him again. Then they led him away to be crucified.

The perversion of the human soul was on display that day. They beat Him until they were tired, they ridiculed Him, spit on Him, faked worship, and they led Him away to be crucified. Jesus suffered this ridicule and shame. They put a purple robe on Him, as if He was a King, but He was a King. He was crucified naked on a cross, a type of punishment that was given to the worst of criminals. But His nakedness covered us and His death delivered us from the penalties of our crimes. The crown of thorns became a crown of life. Satan was happy, Jesus would be killed. I am sure that the demons in hell thought they won and Satan thought he had reclaimed the earth Jesus came to save. How could this powerless Man stop them now? Satan thought he owned the situation, but any situation where Satan seems to rule can be brought down—no weapon prospers against the cross. The love of God overrules Satan every time.

We see in Mark's account of the crucifixion, a man named Simon was called upon to carry His cross.

> [21]And they compel one Simon a Cyrenian, who passed by, coming out of the country, the father of Alexander and Rufus, to bear his cross.

When you go to Jerusalem and follow the Via Dolorosa, or the Street of Sorrows where Jesus carried the cross, you see that a portion of the street is on a downward angle and then it moves upward. Given the beating to Jesus' back, many scholars think it would have been impossible for His muscles to carry the cross up that street again—they had been torn up and destroyed. A man named Simon carried His cross, and will forever be remembered. What an honor to carry His cross.

Sometimes in the middle of our lives, we are asked to carry a burden for another person, a cross, a weight. It is a holy request, and one that bears fruit, for later we will learn that Simon's family was saved. Don't get weary in well doing, for in due season you will reap, if you faint not. It will affect a lot of people. Jesus had to follow that principle too, for that day, His life would be poured out of Him, but it would reap the greatest of crops.

[22]*And they bring him unto the place Golgotha, which is, being interpreted, The place of a skull.* A skull, a death's head, that was a place in Jerusalem and that is a place in us. The earth there is in the form of a skull, and how fitting it was for Christ to be crucified on a portion of the earth like a death's head. It represents the mind that has not been renewed—the deep and depraved nature of man, and the everlasting hatred of the devil. It holds the memories of loss and sorrow. Death was on top that day, but life was on top three days later.

Golgotha was a place of sin, sorrow, and death, it was a place of execution, blood and anguish, a filthy place. Criminals were being executed. Hostile people gathered at the foot of the cross and ridiculed them. Jesus was hung up to die. Nothing beautiful there—move on, or is there. Maybe we should linger here. The Bible talks about the habitations of cruelty, the cruel places of the earth. They exist in the earth now, the cruel prisons, execution walls, pits of bodies, slavery and brutality. Right now the wheels of death are crushing someone. But because of Jesus at that place of cruelty that day, nothing can separate us from the love of God. Love shined bright the day that the sun hid its face.

[23]And they gave him to drink wine mingled with myrrh: but he received it not. Jesus rejected the narcotic that would have taken His pain away.

> *[24]And when they had crucified him, they parted his garments, casting lots upon them, what every man should take, (a prophetic fulfillment of Psalms 22:18) [25]And it was the third hour, and they crucified him. [26]A signboard was fastened to the cross above Jesus' head, announcing the charge against him. It read: "The King of the Jews." [27]Two criminals were crucified with him, their crosses on either side of his. [29]And the people passing by shouted abuse, shaking their heads in mockery. "Ha! Look at you now!" they yelled at him. "You can destroy the Temple and rebuild it in three days, can you? [30]Well then, save yourself and come down from the cross!" [31]The leading priests and teachers of religious law also mocked Jesus. "He saved others," they scoffed, "but he can't save himself! [32]Let this Messiah, this king of Israel, come down from the cross so we can see it and believe him!"*

Even a criminal who was being crucified with Jesus ridiculed him. Everyone mocked Him and said, save Yourself. If You are Who You say You are, why don't You save Yourself.

Everyone was putting down Jesus, the religious rulers, the people who came to mock, the executioners who were Romans, and even one of the criminals who was being crucified. How humiliating is it when people say, where is your God? How humiliating when we were the ones laying hands on the sick, and preaching the sermon and living in holiness, but then find ourselves in a bigger purpose, a

---

higher trial, than we expect that stretches our faith beyond measure. But the mockers are only going to mock so long, because with each believer there is a resurrection. For every death there is a resurrection. Our lives no matter how we see it, if we walk by faith, if we stand in righteousness, is a seed planted that will bear much fruit. We don't know all the fruit that is going to be reaped for eternity.

> [58]Therefore, my beloved brethren, be ye steadfast, unmovable, always abounding in the work of the Lord, forasmuch as ye know that your labor is not in vain in the Lord. I Corinthians 15.
>
> [9]And let us not be weary in well doing: for in due season we shall reap, if we faint not. Galatians 6:9.
>
> [33]At noon, darkness fell across the whole land until three o'clock. [34]Then, at that time Jesus called out with a loud voice, "*EloiEloi, EloiEloi, lemalema sabachthanisabachthani?*" which means, "My God, my God, why have you forsaken me?" Mark 15 (NLT).

Jesus preached seven sermons at the cross. They were short words of His purpose, and His anguish, but I am going to touch on two statements.

First, *My God, why have you forsaken Me?* Never before had Jesus been separated from the Father, from eternity past to the present. Why now? There was no Son without the Father. He was one of the Trinity, of the Godhead. Now He is separated. For a terrible moment in time the Trinity, was split up, the Father and the Holy Spirit were separate from the Son. The Creator was being divided. It is a terrible moment when man does not feel the love of the Father or the power and comfort of the Holy Spirit, but that is the place of all of us before we come to know the Lord, and at times in our walk of faith.

However, that separation is the FINAL PLACE of anyone who rejects Jesus—you will never know the love of the Father or the comfort and power of the Holy Spirit or the grace and truth of the

Son. You may be comforted on earth, with pleasure or rest or money or drugs, but you will never be comforted without the comfort of the Holy Spirit.

The Son was being killed. In a leap of faith, God the Father, God the Son, and God the Holy Spirit, willed this to be so, to display God's love.

How deep the division in our natures, that only God could mend—that God Himself had to be divided up. Why did God forsake Him, because He became sin, and sin separates us from God. Why did the Holy Spirit's comforting presence leave, because the Holy Spirit could not abide with sin. Every time we sin, we are separating ourselves from the source of life, from God. Every time we sin, we are separating ourselves from ourselves, our true identities in Christ, and our true creation, and every time we sin we are separating ourselves from others. We may not know that is happening, but we have an unease in our souls. We hide from ourselves and God. Sin means division, separation, destruction of the true nature. It is devastation.

Next, Jesus felt forsaken, He was doing the will of the Father. Why wasn't the Father there? Because He had to take on our lostness and separation.

Why did God forsake Him? Because there was a bigger purpose, and sometimes when we cry out in our anguish, where are you God, it is because there is a bigger purpose, a purpose to help and redeem others. God is allowing one level of life to die, so another can spring up, pruning for better and greater fruitfulness.

Why did God have to forsake His Son? Because death and sin had to be played out that day. "The wages of sin is death." Romans 6:23. Every sin would have to be taken and met at the cross for us to come into relationship with the Father again. But the essence of sin is separation from God and God could not fellowship with His Son who became sin. Even Jesus could not have relationship with the Father.

My God, My God, why have You forsaken Me? The Father knows that sometimes He has to withdraw from us, to bruise us, so we find a new path forward. It is a departure from all the old paths. He has to cut off the old completely, and here it is at the cross. If He does not bruise us and wound us, we will keep going back to death. If He does not withdraw Himself at times, we would never be desperate to stay in His presence.

My God, My God, why have You forsaken Me? The cross ends sin and its curses. "Christ hath redeemed us from the curse of the law, *being made a curse for us:* for it is written, Cursed is every one that hangs on a tree." Galatians 3:13. The "curse" means alienation from God. That is what it means to be cursed, to be separated from God. He took our curse there, and He will say one day, for those who reject Him: "Depart *from me, ye cursed"* he will say. Matthew 25:41. The curse is *exile* from the presence and glory of God.

Anywhere in our personalities or lives where we reject God, we live under a curse. Many people think that it is all about just being a Christian, or accepting Jesus some time in your life. It is a lot more than that. Jesus lifted the curses off of our lives, by being forsaken by His Father, and therefore we can live in a vital union with Him, and become who He created us to be.

> [35]And some of them that stood by, when they heard *it*, said, Behold, he calleth Elias. [36]And one ran and filled a sponge full of vinegar, and put *it* on a reed, and gave him to drink, saying, Let alone; let us see whether Elias will come to take him down. [37]And Jesus cried with a loud voice, and gave up the ghost.

The end comes—Jesus dies.

The first result recorded in Mark: [38]*And the veil of the temple was rent in twain from the top to the bottom.* We are no longer separated from God. We do not have to go through religious rituals to reach heaven, heaven has reached us. The veil of the temple separated the people from the holy of holies, where the presence of the Lord dwelt in the temple, but now that was all over, the veil was torn. The flesh of Jesus was torn so we could enter His heart, and we forever can go to the throne of grace of God the Father, through the shed blood of Jesus.

We see the first convert after the thief: *[39]And when the centurion, which stood over against him, saw that he so cried out, and gave up the ghost, he said, Truly this man was the Son of God.* The murderer at the foot of the cross is the next convert. This Gentile soldier, who had probably executed hundreds of people, a man with blood on his hands, who had most likely used those hands to put the nails in Jesus' hands and feet, says, truly this was the Son of God.

Can you imagine that the Lord of Glory came from heaven and did this out of love? He hung in the middle of time, between heaven and earth, on behalf of heaven and earth, to absorb the ever widening pool of sin and its effect that continues to burden the planet. He defies time and the control of time. Time was dying that day, as well, and the nature of time is death. Its cumulative penalty was placed on the Son. But He took it so we could have eternal life. He carried our illness, mental, moral and physical, through the stripes on His tattered back.

Jesus said at the cross, "It is *finished.*" What was finished? The devil and his works. He broke the power of rebellion that originated in the throne room of heaven, then trashed creation, and finally disabled and erased man and woman's image, anointing, identity, power and authority at the Garden of Eden. At the cross it was finished, reversed, disassembled, torn down, so the new creation could rise up. He gave us His Person, power, purpose, plan, position, possession, promises, to continue the work He began. He gave us the keys of the kingdom. Satan is under our feet.

What else is finished? We are finished and He is started. Again, everything ends and begins at the cross. We can choose the cross, and there all scores are settled, enemies forgiven, grudges dropped, wounds healed, sins forgiven, sinners released, and demons and sicknesses overcome. Our mothers, fathers, sisters, brothers, friends, betrayers, lovers, haters, are liberated from every tie, lie, definition, distortion, creation that is not based on the blood of Jesus, and the finished work of the cross. The bondages, curses, and patterns of sin for generations are broken, and the false images that we have proudly worn, laid down, like a dirty garment.

The war in our hearts is finished, the war with heaven is finished, and the war on earth is finished, for there is peace on earth by the blood of the cross.

By giving us Himself, He also frees us and finishes vain pursuits that waste our lives and deplete our eternal inheritance.

> (H)ow much more shall the blood of Christ, who through the eternal Spirit offered Himself without spot to God, cleanse your conscience from dead works to serve the Living God. Hebrews 9:13-14.

He became a servant of man to carry the weights of the whole world, so we could be sons and daughters of God to carry the weight of His glory. He traded His life for our death, so we could live His life and carry His person to the world. He reversed our destiny of eternal shame and damnation, so we could receive His eternal inheritance ruling and reigning with Him in this life and forever.

At the cross we can judge ourselves and turn aside the judgment of heaven from us because He took it. We have sinned against heaven and in the sight of others, and if we will but repent, that judgment will be ended. He carried it, He buried it, and He ended it, He defended it in His resurrection. It is finished. We do not have to earn our salvation. He trades His righteousness for our trash, and releases the love and truth to cleanse and restore a planet. But someday the world will no longer be able to avail itself of the communion, the broken body and blood, the divine declaration of love sealed with, "It is finished". The great white throne judgment is the alternative.

CHAPTER FIVE

The Cross is a Place of Crisis

The cross is a place of crisis. Yes, the cross is a place of blood sweat and tears. Everything that is in a man, will pour out of the Man at the cross, everything that is in God, will pour out of the Son of God at the cross. Everything that was in Jesus poured out of Jesus, at the cross—His very blood, every emotion, every hope, every tear, every prophecy, until He stated those final words—It is finished, unto Thy hands I commit My Spirit.

God intended it to be so. At the cross, all that we are on the inside becomes visible. God knows our inner thoughts and motives, our hopes and dreams but we get a chance to reveal them to Him. God the Son exposed God's love at the cross, Jesus was naked, bleeding, crying and dying. We expose our unfaithfulness, nakedness, pain, and bleeding too. It is only then He can solve the deep issues of our lives, the deep stain of sin, the deep pain of brokenness, the crookedness of rebellion, the confusion of mind.

Perhaps you have seen the movie "The Passion of the Christ." Passion means suffering, the suffering of the Christ. But I like to think of passion in the sense of intense love, because only when there is intense love, will someone sacrifice themselves in great suffering, and so our Lord completes His work on earth on the cross. The rest is left to heaven.

Jesus, our lover, gives Himself completely for the world. I thank Jesus, our warrior, for He fights our battle of death, hell, the devil, and sin.

The Bible says a lot about the death of Jesus, because it is very, very important. The life of the world depends on His death. Our very identity as people, our place for eternity, our hopes and the truth of our lives will depend on that death.

His cross is intended to be a sword that cuts deep into the heart of the earth with love. The cross is a place of crisis, both for the Son of God and for us. Jesus was clear about why He came into the world. He knows the scripture that He will be the Seed of a woman to crush the serpent's head. That serpent, Satan, had been contaminating everything on the planet for a long time—corrupting the goodness of God's creation. The poison of sin contaminated our souls, minds, habits, the very dirt we walked on, the realm of nature, and the generations before us and after us.

So it was serious to reverse this mess: This is the reason the Son of God came, that He might undo the works of the devil. I John 3:8. It would take God's blood to atone, or erase and pay the penalty for sin. Jesus knew why He had come. As the time approached for His death, He told His disciples over and over again that it was coming.

> 22For I, the Son of Man, must suffer many terrible things, he said. I will be rejected by the leaders, the leading priests, and the teachers of religious law. I will be killed, but three days later I will be raised from the dead. Luke 9:22 (NLT).

The Bible says that Jesus set His face like flint—His direction was to death, and it required determination. When Peter tries to detour Him into a safer way of living when he learns that Jesus will die, Jesus tells Peter to *get behind Me, Satan.* Matthew 16:22. Satan's way is the way of safety, and self preservation, God's way is the way of surrender and sacrifice. The same choices present themselves to us today. Do we save ourselves or take up our crosses? Do we believe and follow, or disobey and fall? Do we hide somewhere and hope that the challenge, the call, the anointing will pass, or run with it?

Jesus often corrects and chastises His disciples when they do not understand that ruling with God, means sharing in His suffering. James and John are anxious to sit beside Him in His kingdom—they even send their mother on this errand. Who wouldn't want to sit next to Jesus? But it wasn't time for sitting; it was time for following and dying. And wouldn't it be great to enjoy the benefits of the kingdom of God without having to be like Him? Sit up in the high places? But what is the cost? The same cup of suffering that Jesus takes.

He knows the direction He is to take. He tells everyone, they don't understand. All time is compressed for Jesus. In three years, He sets the pattern of truth for the world, the pattern of love for the world, and dies for the sins of the world. He shows His disciples how to minister and to pray, He teaches us the truth of God, the love of God, and the life of God, as He lives it before us. He shows us what true personhood is, as a man or woman. He dies to enable resurrection life after He is gone and give us the gift of the Holy Spirit. He shows the world what God is like on the outside and the inside, and He shows it with grace and truth. He takes the priestly and kingly anointing and imparts it to the people on earth with Him and to His church.

The result of all prayer or intercession on earth is the kingdom, which we see demonstrated and coming about by Jesus. He is giving divine health to those who have sickness, divine direction to the lost, wholeness to the broken, but this is by a holy power, the Holy Spirit. He gives us a pattern so that when we pray, we are bringing a holy power into the natural realm, or the blessedness of God into the cursed realm of the earth. Holy power overcomes unholy power, the world, the flesh and the devil. When we pray we are imposing a new kingdom, over an old, chaotic, sick or unhappy one—He has procured that for us through the cross.

We see that Jesus is not only the Who of the kingdom, but the What of the kingdom and the Way of the Kingdom. He not only demonstrates how the kingdom works, but shows all that our prayers could ever ask for, is seen as He moves in kingdom power and authority. How does Jesus assert divine authority? He teaches them, He casts a demon out and then He heals. He prospers and He loves. So when we pray, we pray with the priestly anointing. In that way the Holy Spirit has control over earthly situations—He opens the floodgates through the cross.

Jesus is at the right hand of the Father ever living to make intercession for us, so that not only we can operate in the kingdom, but release the full realization of what He has procured at the cross on earth as it is in heaven. He is passionate that there should be a complete appropriation of what His blood has paid for. He places all His divinity behind what His divine blood has bought, from taking His blood to the mercy seat in heaven to mediating that blood covenant on earth. That is His place as High Priest until He comes to rule as King.

This all leads to the cross and flows from the cross. The cross is the event that looms before Jesus every day. There is not a break because He knows He is going there and why. He knows in His heart, no matter how much He enjoys life, how much people may love Him, the sweetness of some believers, the fragrance of creation, it is going to be temporary. The whirlwind is coming.

There is no escaping the cross for Jesus, and when we see Him at the Garden of Gethsemane, He is praying to the Father to take this cup from Him. What cup? The cup of suffering and agony and separation without mitigation, the cup of the cross. Is there a way out? There is a crisis before Jesus. He ends by saying, nevertheless, not My will but Thine be done.

The Father does not answer His Son's prayer for escape nor does the Father always answer our prayers for escape—escape from crisis, loneliness, isolation, to a better living situation, freedom from some kind of pain, a bigger life.

An angel is sent to strengthen Jesus, and there He sweats blood. There are times when the Lord just gives us His strength and not avoidance.

There are some things in our lives where He will always give us strength and not avoidance.

There are sins that must be forsaken.

Flesh that has to die.

New ways of thinking and living that have to be understood. We cannot hide from God's will if we are living by faith.

There are places that can only be gained in the walk of faith by suffering. Then we become conquerors.

Jesus is captured and chained, and tried and beaten and crucified, and died. And there is no escaping death, for He says:

> [17]Therefore doth my Father love me, because I lay
> down my life, that I might take it again. [18]No man
> taketh it from me, but I lay it down of myself. I have
> power to lay it down, and I have power to take it
> again. This commandment have I received of my
> Father. John 10:17-18.

The will of Jesus continues with the will of the Father.

And each step that Jesus goes through, He knows what will happen and He knows why, but He doesn't know—because nobody can truly know it until it is experienced—the total, absolute reality and experience of suffering and separation.

We know that the Bible says:

His face was marred more than any man

His beard was plucked out

His back was given to the smiters.

Psalm 22, prophesied of His death, and described crucifixion, a type of execution that did not exist until hundreds of years later. It describes His life being poured out like water, His bones out of joint, His heart like wax, His strength dried up, His tongue dried up, and being brought to the dust of death. Soldiers will gamble for His clothes.

Isaiah 53 tells us that He was despised and rejected of men, a man of sorrows and acquainted with grief. That entitled Him to carry our grief and sorrows, so we would not have to bear the heavy loads beyond our capacity to bear. The rejection included everyone from the thieves beside Him at the cross, to His disciples, Judas, His friend Peter, the religious rulers, the Jewish people, the soldiers who crucified Him, the world, and even Father God and the Holy Spirit, for Father God could not look at the sin He carried.

A crown of thorns adorned His head, and He broke the curses on our lives.

He was hung naked without dignity in front of people who mocked

Him, taking our curses again.

Jesus is in crisis after crisis, can it get any worse, does it ever stop? The sun hides its face, and the Father hides His face, and even Jesus says, *My God, My God Why have You forsaken Me?*

The cross is a place for crisis for Jesus, because although He knows the glory that will happen afterwards, and although He knows that this is the only way to save the world, <u>the test is hard and the climb is steep.</u> It is one thing to talk about it and another to live it.

And folks, because the test is hard and the climb was steep for Jesus, He paved the way with all our hard tests and steep climbs. No climb was so high or sublime as His. Thank God He went before us and did it for us.

The cross was also a place of crisis for everyone around Jesus the day He died.

He knows it is going to get bad, and He prepares the hearts of His disciples—let not your heart be troubled, you believe in God, believe also in Me. John 14:1. *All hell is going to break loose and I want you to know that I have prepared the way to heaven—this is how, and I am going before you.*

It was time of crisis for the people who wanted Him dead. Judas plunges himself into the bottomless pit of evil. The chief rulers and priests conspired, paid off Judas, got false witnesses, riled up the mob, dragged Him to trial after trial, had meetings, met with Pilate, had trials—it was exhausting to get rid of the Son of God. Will this Jesus ever get out of their planet and stop bothering them? How do we rid ourselves of truth? His power and authority are annoying and reduces their power and authority. How do we get rid of this man? How can we stop Him from showing up and revealing us as frauds? It is not so easy to murder a prophet. How do we keep things as they are? How do we stay on top?

Everyone involved embraces the lie and the Liar, and engages in two incomprehensible betrayals: Betrayal of God Himself and betrayal of the human race created in the image of God.

It is a place of crisis for Pontius Pilate. The scripture tells us that he wanted to let Jesus go, but to do the Jews a favor, he not only had

Him brutally beaten, but executed Him. Well, I don't want to do the wrong thing, but these people are forcing me, and I have to think of my position, and my place as a ruler here. He compromises because he is unable to act on the truth, even with the warning of his wife's prophetic dream. That was a pretty big favor, getting rid of the Son of God.

It is a place of crisis for His friends and family. Peter denies Him three times, and the rest of the disciples scatter. His mother pitifully looks on with the other women as her son died. When the going gets tough, do you stick beside Him? I don't know if I could. I am not going to imagine myself so brave. It is only by the power of the Holy Spirit that I can stand now.

It is even a time of crisis for the earth—the sun hides its face, there is an earthquake. There has to be some anguish felt in creation the day the Creator died. Creation itself, which is held together by the power of His word, was totally distressed, pained and confused when the Word itself died. What *on earth* was happening? The earth quaked—when men did not. The sun hid its face, when men should have.

It is a place of crisis for the divine Holy Spirit, He must depart from the Son because of sin.

Finally there is crisis even for the Father God. Just as Abraham offered his son, the Father's Son, His only begotten Son, is the sacrifice. But this time, the death came. *Someone, some innocent, eternal, holy, One, ultimately had to die to stop the cycle of death and hell and the grave for us to have eternal life—there was no further ram in the bush.* God begins things and God ends things. There is finality. His Son, His beloved Son was at the end of Abraham's crisis, and, He would have to turn His face away. They had been together for eternity past, and waited many long years for this day. They had never been separated. They had fellowshipped and planned the creation of the world, and at that same time, planned for His death, He was the Lamb slain from the foundation of the world. There it is, the day Christ died, and He cannot look at His Son because He is covered with the sins of all of us, all our filth was on Him. And the Holy Spirit must withdraw. How painful. God so loved.

Everybody's heart was being tested that day, and everybody's heart still is, because of the cross. If you think that isn't true, think of all the controversy around the world for believing in Jesus Christ. Crosses are hidden and broken and the true cross is rejected and mocked.

There is no escaping the cross for Jesus, and as we hear of this event, open our ears to the preaching of its truth, there is no escaping that event for us. We cannot ignore the cross, because to ignore the cross, would mean to ignore God, and Jesus, and His claims on our lives. As I wrote, there is no God without the cross.

> [16]For God so loved the world, that he gave his only begotten Son, that whosoever believeth in him should not perish, but have everlasting life. John 3:16.

We cannot shortcut the cross. There is no other name under heaven given among men whereby we must be saved.

The preaching of the cross is foolishness to the natural man, but it is salvation to those who believe.

We cannot shortcut the cross in our own lives, for we must take up our crosses daily and die to self and follow Him, this is the only way to create sons and daughters of God. He died on His cross, so we could take up ours.

Those who ignore the cross of Jesus do so at the risk of their eternity, and those who ignore the cross they must carry in their own lives, do so at the risk of the abundant life and the promises and purposes of God in their lives.

The cross is a place of crisis for us. We are invited there every day to trust God, when all hell seems to be winning. We are called to trust when the flesh is weary of obedience. We are called to forgive as He does, and keep forgiving.

There is crisis when God does not seem to answer prayers—God didn't answer Jesus' prayers that day either, but it was because of a bigger plan. Sometimes there are prayers to save ourselves that are not answered, because His more important work of making new creatures is being accomplished. And because He is also the

God of the resurrection, and if there are no crosses, there are no resurrections.

The cross places pressure on us, and that pressure is good, because it is pressure for God and from God. It forces us to make decisions and be accountable. Without it we would have no way of knowing God, of knowing that God loves us, or that we love Him, knowing ourselves and our required response to ourselves and others, or that we need to be accountable to Him. It is daily proof of a God Who is in us and for us.

The cross is the golden standard of love and truth. There we humbly surrender ourselves and yield to His finished work of eternal love.

However, when we receive the gift of the cross, the struggle is over, for we have entered in. And when we live out the cross the struggle is less, for His yoke is easy and His burden light.

> 8But God showed his great love for us by sending Christ to die for us while we were still sinners. 9And since we have been made right in God's sight by the blood of Christ, he will certainly save us from God's judgment. 10For since we were restored to friendship with God by the death of his Son while we were still his enemies, we will certainly be delivered from eternal punishment by his life. 11So now we can rejoice in our wonderful new relationship with God— all because of what our Lord Jesus Christ has done for us in making us friends of God. Romans 5 (NLT).

The cross is not just a place of crisis, it is a place of truth, safety in the love of God, salvation, cleansing, healing, deliverance. It is the door of life for the world, that old rugged cross, and while it is ridiculed by the world, so rude, so crude, but it is so refined, divine and sublime. And He did it just for you and me.

> O the depth of the riches both of the wisdom and knowledge of God! how unsearchable are his judgments, and his ways past finding out! Romans 11:33 (NKJV).

The cross is our door to a new life—there we find all the opportunities of heaven, and leave the sadness of the earth behind. We find the Father, Son and Holy Spirit, and eternity. Without crosses, there are no resurrections, so you are asked to come to the foot of the cross, and believe and receive.

Free men and women are only made at the cross. There are no manufactured products there, no class in school, no mysterious religion, wild living, incredible drug, new country, new person, new marriage, new movie, or no other place that guarantees freedom.

It is that straight and narrow gate where we can leave all our baggage—everything that we carry in this world and was loaded on us when we were born, and become truly who God created us to be. It is there where we leave ourselves and belong to God. Because it is there we have the chance to become like the Son of God himself.

Thank you Jesus. Thank you for the cross, my Friend.[1]

---

1 From "Once Again" by Matt Redman, © Copyright 1996 Thankyou Music (PRS) (admin. worldwide by EMI CMG Publishing excluding Europe which is admin. by kinswaysongs.com).

Part II

A Revelation of the Cross

CHAPTER SIX

Straight is the Gate

> Enter ye in at the strait gate: for wide is the gate, and broad is the way, that leadeth to destruction, and many there be which go in thereat: [14]Because strait is the gate, and narrow is the way, which leadeth unto life, and few there be that find it. Matthew 7:13-14.

Straight is the gate and narrow is the way. This gate does not lead to destruction, but to life. It is a timeless gate, a humble gate, the only gate. It is the gate Jesus is and was and always will be, and the gate He took. That gate is the cross.

The gate of the cross is the first step on the road to glory, and the only way we can be transformed from sons of men to sons of God. God chose the cross for His only begotten Son to reconcile the world to Himself, and He chooses the cross for those who would be sons of glory and reconcile themselves to God.

At the departure gate of the cross we leave our life, our identity, our possessions, our sins, our justification, our denial, our pride, our sickness, our failures, goals, age, family, power and powerlessness, pleasures and sorrows, time and waste, the world and its visions, and betroth ourselves to Jesus. We leave our hopes, good works, and our goodness, for these must die and be transformed. All that is not eternal dies there; everything that brought sickness or joy, for we are entering a new type and dimension of life, from a marriage to this world, to marriage with the Son of God, the Bridegroom, Who purchased us with His own blood from the slavery of sin. We must respond to the demands of this new life, leaving the earthly home of our earthly fathers to be joined with Christ and the Heavenly Father, strangely—in the most earthly and degrading of events—an execution.

We leave our garments of destruction or pride and put on robes of righteousness, the pure garments of those who would join themselves to the Savior. We take His name, His family, His suffering, His cross, His life, His commandments, His death. We are betrothed to a new Husband. That ring of authority that we gain by dying to self and living unto God, gained in the name of the Son Who has all authority in heaven and on earth, is also our wedding ring to Him. No marriage, no unity, no sonship, no inheritance, no authority: Be faithful, servant, son, daughter, friend, wife, the blessings come with relationship and obedience.

The straight gate of the cross is the door to life itself, as it cleanses from sin, bears grief and sickness, and produces power over Satan, because we are no longer subject to sin and its immediate or generational effect. We become eternal beings, and the power of the cross reaches from eternity past to eternity present to eternity future. We gain the authority of the Crucified One, Who had no sin, for He has power on earth to forgive sins, by His stripes we are healed, and principalities, powers, rulers of the darkness of this world, demonic hosts are under His feet.

The cross is the table set before us in the presence of our enemies, disguised to the world as something despicable and foolish, but mighty unto God. There we die to the limited resources of self and the world and are united with the unlimited resources of the kingdom of God. It is the feast of the kingdom, prepared by the King.

"For other foundation can no man lay than that is laid which is Jesus Christ." I Corinthians 3:11. God will not build on a faulty foundation. He will not create sons and daughters on human foundations. The cross tears down the foundation of the human race, so the children of God and the kingdom of God may be raised on the Chief Cornerstone, Jesus.

The cross strips away and strips away as long as we are on this planet. The old is stripped away and kingdoms of darkness dismantled on the altars of our hearts. As suddenly, the new can emerge and we can see and be what is real. Jesus was stripped of every earthly thing and His glory at the cross. This was the other Mount of Transfiguration for Him, the way He received the coming joy and glory set before Him; and it is the Mount of Transfiguration for us. This is because at the cross, that which is holy and eternally real shines through, in Him and in us. We learn that "God is love" I John 4:8, and "God so loved the world that He gave His only begotten Son, that whosoever believeth in Him, should not perish but have everlasting life." John 3:16. God by His personality and in His mercy strips away that which is false in our lives, so the truth will be made manifest in our mortal bodies, so we may be doers of the Word, as Jesus, the Ultimate Doer of the Word.

The cross is the heartbeat at the center of this planet, it is the body of Christ exposed to the world--Jesus inside out, His blood cleansing and pulsing out to give life to the world. So, too, the Body of Christ, the church, will be exposed to the world as it goes to the cross, when, in its foolishness, it dies to self in obedience to God. Then Jesus again and again will be lifted up, and the world will see. They will see God's love. They will only see God's love when we die. It is there they will see the straight gate. They will see.

The world understands death more than life. Its hours are counted in anticipation of death. Money, possessions, power, pleasure, are measured by the hour and the second to hold off the inevitable. They are acquired to fend off the dreaded day, to glorify time and self. The world tries to fix death—you cannot fix death. The world does not understand our joys, the ecstasy of the Spirit or the strength of the doer, but they will respond to our dying to self on which they place such great price and pride in their own lives. Death is not the same enemy to us.

The cross is a place of unplanned strategy to the world, but the ways and will of God. Straight is the gate and narrow is the way because we are preordained to good works which can only be fulfilled if we fit God's eternal time schedule of divine moments and interventions, the orbit of the Eternal Spirit of God, leading we know not where, the clock in which we are the hands directed by His holiness and compassion.

Straight is the gate because the power and anointing promised is only attained by walking through the gate and being cleansed. Purity and simplicity alone yield to the gentle wind of the Spirit. There are no formulas, only the will of God, the meat of the servant.

All others are left outside the straight and narrow gate. Outside that gate are adulterers and whoremongers, and those who love to lie. They abide outside the heavenly gate because they did not enter through the gate of the cross.

Enter into the straight gate. There is no place else to go on this planet for true life.

CHAPTER SEVEN

Jesus at the Jordan

Then Jesus came from Galilee to John at the Jordan to be baptized by him. And John tried to prevent Him, saying, "I need to be baptized by You, and are You coming to me?" But Jesus answered and said to him, "Permit it to be so now, for thus it is fitting for us to fulfill all righteousness." Then he allowed Him. When He had been baptized, Jesus came up immediately from the water; and behold, the heavens were opened to Him, and he saw the Spirit of God descending like a dove and alighting upon Him. And suddenly a voice came from heaven, saying, "This is my beloved Son, in whom I am well pleased." Matthew 3:13-17.

And John bore witness saying, "I saw the Spirit descending from heaven like a dove, and He remained upon Him. I did not know Him, but He who sent me to baptize with water said to me, 'Upon whom you see the Spirit descending, and remaining on Him, this is He who baptizes with the Holy Spirit.' And I have seen and testified that this is the Son of God." John 1:32-34.

This is the most important of events. Next to the cross and the resurrection, the baptism of Jesus at the Jordan and the events that follow in the days of testing and temptation are the foundation of Jesus' ministry and all ministry and life in the Spirit.

Jesus came to the Jordan River to be baptized by John. This was the beginning of His ministry and the beginning of a new dispensation, the dispensation of grace. Jesus was identified by John the Apostle as being full of grace and truth, and of His fullness we have all received. John 1:14,16.

John the Baptist's identification of Jesus is most significant because the baptism of Jesus in the Jordan marks the end of the law and the beginning of the cross, a cross concealed in the waters of a river meant for sinners and a baptism He did not need. The law came by Moses, but then, one day, grace and truth came by Jesus Christ. God was no longer focusing on what we had done, good or bad, but what He would do under grace. A new covenant of redemption would be cut by God Himself. The divine transition was prophesied at the Jordan that day; the Passover was to be over, and the cross established. The time of looking forward had ceased; the Promised Seed was here, Who would crush the serpent's head. John identified Jesus as "The Lamb of God Who takes away the sin of the world," and there at the Jordan the Lamb demonstrated why He came to a fallen race in one small capsule of time.

The Jordan is a place of death and life. This is God's order, and always will be. It is a place of departure, leaving an old life behind. The examples in the Old Testament are many, the children of Israel coming into the Promised Land, Elisha following Elijah, Naaman's healed life and transition to faith, and more. After the Jordan, a new dimension of life is promised. The natural mind thinks of life, then death. We say, "I will live my live and then die." This reasoning is for those who say "I will live *my* life." But God tells us *we will die and then live*, His life and ours through Him. Likewise, the Jordan is a place of baptism unto death and baptism unto life, for those who are born of the water and the Spirit.

The Jordan was a place of departure for Jesus. He was departing from His life in quiet growth with the Father, and beginning His ministry and ultimately His sacrifice. The Jordan had prophetic significance to Jesus. Jesus died before He went to the cross. He died to all He was in heaven where He came from, to establish the kingdom of heaven where He was going to. Then He died to an earthly family so He could establish a heavenly one. If Jesus had not died beforehand, before the foundation of the world, He could not have gone to the cross. He died to the privileges and power of His Sonship, so we could ascend to them. He died to heaven with the Father so we could go to heaven with the Father. He died to glory so we could have glory. His coming to earth, and His baptism at the Jordan are memorial altars of departure speaking as witnesses of that truth. He took the seed of Adam and became one of us, tasting death for all and fulfilling the cup of that bitterness—the meaning of the first baptism. The old man/woman dies. He died and died and died and then died.

The Jordan represents a place in the spirit where we all must be birthed, cleansed and baptized. There, old lives, old dispensations, and old orders end, and new lives are founded in Christ Jesus and energized by the Holy Spirit by the will of the Father. Lives under the dominion of Satan are buried in a symbolic death and raised in symbolic resurrection to life under the dominion of the Godhead. The baptism of the Jordan is the entire plan of redemption.

Jesus came to be baptized by John, but Jesus did not need to be cleansed at the Jordan River. Here is our first key. He was not a sinner, and no repentance was due. There was no mar on His character, and He was the owner of the kingdom of heaven, and not a receiver. But He did come to identify with sinners, humbly taking their sin, penalty, and judgment to fulfill God's method of dealing with sin. He took our sickness, death, brokenness, and feebleness with which we struggle, in all ways saving His creation, lapsed in failure and limitation because of sin.

Jesus tells John to "permit it to be so" to fulfill all righteousness. But how does Jesus fulfill all righteousness? First, He understood the that innocent would suffer for the guilty, as innocent blood had been shed for centuries under the law. Second, He walked and talked the law of love in His ministry, as both the Holy One and Lawgiver. Third, in this instant of time, the baptism points to a death on the cross that would absorb all the penalties and curses of the law and impart to us His righteousness, so that fourthly, we could thereafter fulfill the law and righteousness until He comes again.

Without John's understanding, Jesus allows Himself to be buried in the waters of death, pointing to the cross to come. John's natural mind still could not grasp the One before him or the reason for the baptism. He prophesied of the fullness and the mission of the Lamb of God, but he did not experientially know it. John could not know that in Him all of the old nature from Adam dies, and in Him all the new nature in the second Adam, Christ Jesus lives. This is the first half of the baptism.

However, we see another great picture as Jesus emerges from the water to be filled with the Holy Spirit. As we know Jesus was baptized in the Holy Spirit when He came out of the waters of death. Emptying Himself unto death by the hands of man, then, in the form of a man, He is filled with the fullness of God by the Holy Spirit. This second baptism displays the infilling of the new man and woman in Christ Jesus with the Holy Spirit. These new ones are no longer empowered by sin, or the flesh, or the devil or the world, for such men and women have gone to the cross. They are filled with the power of the Holy Spirit, just as Jesus is and was.

When Jesus arose from the water, the heavens were opened. John saw the Spirit of God descending on Him, and staying there. Lastly, the Father says, "This is my beloved Son in Whom I am well pleased." If we have gone to the cross, can't we expect the same from the Father? The answer is yes, for the cross, first of all, wipes out the impossible distance between the Father and fallen men and women, because old lives have died and new lives are resurrected in the image of His dear Son. Finally we are filled with the same power as Jesus Christ.

The heavens are opened. We can hear the Father, His heart is open, and we can see the work of the Holy Spirit, just as John did. There, love and truth, the divine pair, are united in the humble obedience of Jesus to the glory of God the Father, Son and Holy Spirit, and the Father is well pleased.

Who was at the baptism of Jesus? All the great witnesses were there:

> For there are three that bear record in heaven, the
> Father, the Word, and the Holy Ghost: and these

three are one. And there are three that bear witness
on earth, the Spirit, and the water and the blood,
and these three agree in one. I John 5:7-8.

The Father, the Son, and the Holy Spirit, the three Who bear record in heaven, were there. All the great witnesses of God's redemption of the earth were there, the Spirit, the water, and the blood, for the regenerative work of the Spirit, the cleansing power of the water and the blood were there demonstrated in the baptism.

Heaven and earth were in total agreement in that moment—for the monumental introduction, release and impartation of the Son of God on earth for His redemptive work. There were other witnesses. The greatest prophet of the Old Testament participated in prophetically ending his dispensation and starting another. There was a crowd of witnesses. The Lamb Himself, the Witness of the truth and Messenger of the Covenant, joined us all together eternally. Common people were witnesses and detractors were witnesses, and we, who journey the path of the cross, are witnesses 2000 years later, with our own cloud of witnesses.

Each baptism has an agent. Human hands are the agent of baptism with water. For at the hands of all of us came the cross. But God is the baptizer in the Holy Spirit. Having emptied Himself of His essential power as the Second Person of the Trinity, He becomes a man receiving power from above. That day the Holy Spirit descends on Him and does not leave, just as the Holy Spirit would do so in the upper room after Jesus left to empower the church. By then, they knew and began to live the message of the cross.

The baptism of the cross will be by human hands, but the baptism of the Holy Spirit is only by divine hands; it is a part of Jesus and us that is cut without human hands, making us part of that Rock cut out of the mountain that will destroy all the kingdoms of the earth. Daniel 2:34. The cuts of the cross will be by human hands. In fact, we kill ourselves unknowingly. But the baptism of the Holy Spirit was by divine hands. The baptism of the cross brings the death of the old, sinful and counterfeit in humanity, for the old is done away with. But the baptism of the Holy Spirit presses us into a new life and the kingdom.

Although He was without sin, a prior existence ended for Jesus, as seen in the baptism. His former life would be transformed as He took the form of a servant and became like us. He would always be the Son of God, the Second Person of the Trinity, but He would live in the resurrected body of a man. Although He had all the power of heaven before He came to earth, He emptied Himself and received it anew again showing us how to obtain it and live it. Likewise, the baptism of the Holy Spirit gives us power to become sons and daughters of God.

We go to the Jordan with Jesus. There we experience the cross by our own hands and by the hands of many others through the will of the Father. Sometimes we come to the cross through our own repentance, clinging to the Savior. We leave our needs, sorrows, sickness, sin, and self at the cross. Sometimes others will take us to the cross in persecution and hardship and oppressive circumstances. In such cases we take up our crosses daily and follow Him. But do not go to the cross without the resurrection, for Jesus comes to us as the Baptizer in the Holy Spirit and fire. He declares: "But ye shall receive power, after that the Holy Ghost is come upon you; and ye shall be witnesses unto me both in Jerusalem and in all Judea and in Samaria and unto the uttermost part of the earth." Acts 1:8. Through the baptism of the Holy Spirit we take on His cloak of authority and power and newness of life.

Our sins, the world and the forces of darkness are the agents of the cross for us. God allowed it for His only begotten Son, and He allows it for us, so we may be conformed into His image. God allows the counterfeit kingdoms of the world to bring their own destruction. But God comes in a mighty swoop to open heaven, pour out His Spirit upon us, and place His loving seal of approval upon us: "This is my beloved son and daughter in whom I am well pleased."

In the days that followed His baptism, Jesus would be driven into the wilderness by the Holy Spirit, tested by God and tempted by the devil. Again, Jesus experiences the cross before the cross. If Jesus had not been tested by the Father to the extreme and tempted by the devil to the extreme, as an offering released into the wilderness, He could not have set His face like flint to go to the cross. Despite the offer by the god of this world to give Jesus the kingdoms of this world by worshiping him, Jesus would decline the offer and gain the kingdoms of this world through the cross—ruling in heaven and earth. Had Jesus accepted Satan's offer and obtained the kingdoms of this world without the cross, Jesus would have become the Antichrist, instead of the Christ. Jesus would have ruled the world under Satan, obtained all the kingdoms of this world like the Antichrist, salvation would have stopped, the plan of God ended, and the world set up for destruction. Just as when the real Antichrist comes, salvation will stop with the mark of the Beast, and the world will be destroyed. And how many potential world rulers have bowed or will bow their knee, how many people have traded the kingdom of heaven for the kingdom of earth, so that they could be on top of that unholy mountain for a while?

But Jesus did not bow His knee and never would—His meat was to do the will of His Father, and given this experience in the wilderness, Satan should have guessed the final outcome then and there. And here again, the tempting was simply just folded into the test, because the message of the cross is folded into the tempting by Satan.

CHAPTER EIGHT

The Incorruptible Seed

God's love letter to the human race
Jesus Christ, the living Word
Filled the world with truth and grace
And cancelled its deep disgrace.

Ought not Christ to have suffered these things, and to enter into His glory? Luke 24:26.

But some man will say, How are the dead raised up? and with what body do they come? Thou fool, that which thou sowest is not quickened, except it die: And that which thou sowest, thou sowest not the body that shall be, but bare grain, it may chance of wheat, or of some other grain... So also is the resurrection of the dead. It is sown in corruption; it is raised in incorruption... It is sown a natural body; it is raised a spiritual body. There is a natural body, and there is a spiritual body. I Corinthians 15:35-37, 42, 44.

For this corruptible must put on incorruption, and the mortal must put on immortality. So when this corruptible shall have put on incorruption, and this mortal shall have put on immortality, then shall be brought to pass the saying that is written, Death is swallowed up in victory. I Corinthians 15:53-54.

Being born again, not of corruptible seed, but of incorruptible, by the word of God which liveth and abideth forever. I Peter 1:23.

The incorruptible seed is the word, and the incorruptible seed is the Word. God had settled it from the very beginning that each seed would reproduce life after its own kind, and all of spiritual and natural life is founded on this principle.

In the beginning God created man and woman in His image and likeness, but in the Garden, the incorruptible seed of God was aborted as Satan sowed the "unword" in the heart of man and woman and they ate of the tree of the knowledge of good and evil, losing their glory and authority as sons and daughters of God. And so the dilemma of reproducing sons and daughters of God was created again.

The scriptures say that in the heart of God was a seed. This seed was the Lamb slain from the foundation of the world; and in the heart of God that Seed would be sown at the proper time first in the womb of Mary, then in the experience of men, then in the womb of the earth, then in the hearts of men. The full potential of that Seed could only be expressed in part by the anointed prophets of God, who described the glory of God filling the earth, a millennial reign, a new heaven and new earth, the manifestation of the sons of God, and heaven itself. Eye hath not seen and ear hath not heard all that the one Seed, Jesus, would reproduce.

"Thy kingdom come, thy will be done." The incorruptible Seed could not reproduce the incorruptibility, the durability, the eternity, the glory, the life of God, until He was buried in the earth. Jesus planted heaven on earth and joined heaven to earth eternally. God put His eternal stake into this earth by the cross—we are reconciled.

He planted it as He went about doing good, and healing all those oppressed of the devil. He softened their hearts up by doing good, but then He demonstrated the kingdom of heaven, something only the power of God could do. Yet, the incorruptible Seed of God could not reproduce its incorruptibility overcoming the last enemy death, and all the other enemies, Satan, self, sickness, sin, culminating in death and hell, until Jesus died and was sown in the earth, and rose again in resurrection life. Because He planted heaven on earth, each time our earthly hearts receive the seed, the seed will reproduce God and His kingdom, for the restoration of God's authority in us and through us. An eternal God reproduces eternal life, that very dimension of life that gives us the potential to be sons and daughters of God, for which fame, fortune and love aspire, but only have temporary effect.

Ought not Christ to have suffered these things and to have entered into His glory? The seed is sown in dishonor. The seed itself gives no outward indication of its potential. The seed is hidden in the earth, and its potential is hidden in the earth. It is sown in corruptible form. The seed is bare and naked and isolated, not at all pretty or desirable. Only in the vision of the Creator is its total potential of the seed understood and released. The Seed of Jesus was subject to the hands of man and left to die where man willed, it seemed, and buried where man willed. That Seed was not beautiful, it had no comeliness that we should desire it. It was literally a bare seed, for the Seed had been stripped of His glory, power, and authority, and was covered with the dirt of the world.

Evil men denied Life itself, when they buried that Seed. Yet didn't they know that you can't kill God, and that life would spring forth out of the earth—a glorious, magnificent, supernatural, eternal, life? Had they walked with Him, instead of against Him, they might have understood the revelation that Jesus gave His disciples of Himself in the Psalms, and Moses, and the prophets on the road to Emmaus. The suffering was the dishonor and reproach that enabled the resplendent glory later, as Jesus was quickened by the power of God. So we, like Jesus, are sown in corruption, and raised in incorruption, sown in a natural body, but raised in a spiritual body. We are clothed in His resurrection. His death released the harvest of the world to God.

Jesus said,

Unless a corn of wheat fall into the ground and die, it
abideth alone; but if it die, it bringeth forth much fruit.
He that loveth his life shall lose it; and he that hateth
his life in this world shall keep it unto life eternal.
John 12:24-25.

As stated previously the natural mind reasons that there is life,
then death, but God's order is always death, then life; we die to one
life and one kingdom to live to another. We shed the shell of this
earth, to enter into the glory of the kingdom of heaven. We leave our
earthly fathers and mothers, that which has shaped or bent us, and
spring forth in resurrection life of greater and greater glory. Jesus
had to fall into the ground and die, so a crop could be released of
sons and daughters of God. How else could God reproduce His
nature? Love is to die, to die to self, pride, designs, plans, hopes,
fears, addictions, sin, so a new nature can be reproduced in the image
and pattern of the Son of God. Jesus died so a harvest of the world
could spring up, living and walking and dying and living as He did.

At the cross, the mockers said, "He saved other, let him save
himself, if he be Christ, the chosen of God." One of the thieves
said, "If thou be the Christ, save thyself and us." Luke 23: 35, 39.
The chief priests and scribes said, "Let Christ the King of Israel
descend now from the cross, that we may see and believe." Mark
15:32. Here's the problem: They had to *see* to believe at *their* time
and in *their* way, choosing *their* own methods for validation of His
divinity. To them true power was an avoidance of death, instead of
an overcoming of it. The fact of the matter was, because He was the
Christ He stayed on the cross, and did not avoid it.

Still later when Jesus cried, "Eloi, Eloi, lama sabathani?" it was
interpreted that He was calling on Elijah to save Him and take Him
down from the cross. Yet the truth of the matter was that Jesus had
conversed with Moses and Elijah on the Mount of Transfiguration
about His death, not His escape. The Mount of Transfiguration was
the reverse side of Mount Calvary. Three men were on that Mount
also, one representing the law, and one representing the prophets,
and One fulfilling both. Two men represented the word of God,
but the Man in the center was the Word, the covenant of life itself.

Instead of thieves at His right and left hand, two divinely appointed witnesses stood at His side, men who had been used of God to bring restoration from the fall, until Jesus came. There the Son of God was glorified, shining. At the cross, a Savior hung, dying, bearing sin, pain and shame, surrounded by thieves simply representing the saved or the lost. How the leaders and their followers tried to drag Him down, discredit Him, take away His anointing and favor, deny His divinity. What a failure to apprehend the nature of His glory. Pure evil is so destructive and ignorant.

All three men at the Mount of Transfiguration represented the resurrection. Moses had died, but his body was never found. There was no grave for Moses. In Moses was the hidden potential of the law, providing a platform to bring a Savior to birth a resurrected race. Elijah never died, but ascended to heaven in a chariot of fire. Here was a prophetic illustration and vision of the resurrection and the translation of the church. There was no grave for Elijah. Then there was Jesus, the Son of Man, Who died and rose again, fulfilling the law and the prophets, and more, creating a new race of born again people who would one day have resurrection bodies and dwell in eternal life. Jesus burst open the grave. No grave could hold Him. He died, yet He lived. He descended, yet He ascended.

Had the Pharisees understood the law and the prophets they would have understood the Man on the cross before them. But, in fact, Jesus came to earth to be that hidden Seed. From the very beginning His glory was disguised. Jesus had to die, or there would be no crop; and now there is one that will never stop. Without the cross, His death and burial and resurrection, there could be no new heaven or new earth or new men and women to populate the vastness of God's creation. Without the cross God could not have recreated anything or anyone. And without the cross we would have stayed in darkness for eternity.

CHAPTER NINE

Heaven and Hell

Heaven and hell met at the cross
The heaven of God's love
And the hell of our sin
Love won a stunning victory.

Heaven and hell met at the cross. In one sense it was the ultimate showdown between Satan's counterfeit kingdom, power, glory and authority, and God's kingdom, power, glory and authority, to determine who controlled planet Earth. It was a conflict that started at the throne room of God when Lucifer was expelled, and continued with man and woman in the Garden of Eden, when Satan, first seduced Adam and Eve to despise their birthright, by rejecting the will of their Creator. And second, it was a conflict that raged on because Satan did not want to lose his dominion on earth through any man, woman or child, who God had created in His image to exercise dominion. The outlaw from heaven in hatred, anger, and retaliation against God had waged a long fight. In the Garden God's created son Adam, Luke 3:38, lost eternal life in fellowship with the Father, and lived from then on as a sinner out of the center of his own will. At the cross, Jesus reversed the disaster.

When the Lord prophesied that the "Seed of the woman" would crush the head of the serpent in overturning his authority, the forces of hell pursued who they thought was the intended "seed of the woman," Abel, and caused him to be murdered by Cain. When another son, Seth, was born to Adam and Eve, Satan then set out to contaminate the human race. When the human race was destroyed by the flood, only righteous Noah and his family carried the human lineage to the Messiah. To carry on God's appointed plan, Abraham was called to be faithful to God, waiting for the promised son with his barren wife well into their old age, twenty years after receiving the promise. Moses was given the law to preserve a people for God and the Messiah, but the Jewish people carelessly broke it. The family line of the Christ was to be carried through the house of David and yet Satan *nearly* succeeded in destroying or degrading the kings of Judah so the Messiah could not be born through the line of David, despite the law given to uphold the righteousness of God's people. At his birth, His mother and Joseph were thrown into a national census, an upheaval dislocating them from familiar surroundings, and probably causing acute distress to Mary. Herod murdered many babies in the area to destroy this new King. As His earthly ministry began, Satan tried to seduce Him into obtaining the kingdoms, power and glory that Satan had, without the plan of God. Ignorant and evil men dogged Him in His ministry and claimed His birthright, power and authority were not of God. They tried to discredit Him, called Him a blasphemer and deceiver, implied He was born of fornication, and eventually put Him to death through phony trials and lying witnesses. Hell was displayed in cruel mocking and scourging by sinners, who stripped Him and beat Him so there was no beauty in Him that we should desire Him. At last, the death of Jesus at the cross, was to be the final blow to God's plan to regain His creation. In this the forces of hell conjectured, in evil stupidity and hatred, that they could stop the rulership of God on this earth. And so, the cross stands as that one place where hell seems to gain ascendancy over earth and the plans of God—for Satan has always wanted his kingdom to come and his will to be done. However, as we know, hell's plans were only God's strategy for victory.

A curious thing happened. In another way hell came to view that day. This is where the heaven convergence awesomely enters. It came into view when our Lord took upon Himself all of our sins, sorrows, sicknesses, grief, iniquities, curses, and the essence of human bondage that is the expression of hell on earth, and that which would usher the way for the human race, past, present, and future, to be condemned for eternity to hell. He took the judgment and penalty of sin, and sin itself on Himself as the Ultimate Sacrifice.

Hell was at the cross. This disgorging of hell was hurled at Jesus, Who carried it, but then buried it all in the grave. When He arose, the power of this sin and bondage died and was broken also for time and eternity because it had no eternal life residing in it. Heaven and hell will always meet at the cross. Satan exulted to see the Son of God murdered by sinful men and women, but did not know that death, its ugliness and pain, sin and self, disfiguration, sickness, sorrow, and Satan himself would be uprooted and dethroned there, by the Man who would carry the keys of death and hell. Satan still cheers when sons and daughters of God face their own crosses, but experience should tell him that the more crosses there are, the more resurrected children of God there will be. The cross and the resurrection are branded into us, life more abundantly; supernatural, overcoming, and eternal.

Heaven was at the cross that day, too, in another way; the heaven of God's love was displayed. God, who so loved the world, His creation, that He gave His only begotten Son--the only Son ever begotten by God the Father to live on this earth, the only Son who was the complete visible expression of the Father God—that whosoever rich, poor, of whatever race, young, old, sick, maimed, depraved, sorrowful, lost, in, out, up or down, believed in Him, should not perish, but have the dimension of everlasting life incorporated into their very being, a uniting and consolidation that could never be taken from them, for it had no human origin and was not subject to human violation. So heaven's gift to the world was at the cross that day. That which is eternally real was at the cross. That unique act of love by which the Son of God was stripped of His glory, is the very act by which we can obtain the glory of the only begotten of the Father, obtain a greater glory than was lost in Eden, and become sons and daughters of God.

God's love, which is the currency of the kingdom of heaven, and the life of His Son, was lavishly spent at this table, the cross, set before us in the presence of our enemies. The bread and the wine, the simple bits of common substance, sanctified and made holy as emblems of our communion with God, is the most expensive meal in the history of the universe. Our communion should always keep us in humility of the realization of the love of God.

In heaven pure love dwells. At the cross, pure love was released to the earth. It is and was released in the river of cleansing life that flows from the side of our Lord to wash away our sins. It is and was released in the broken body by which we obtain healing for our sickness and sorrow.

The literal body of Christ was most exposed to the world at the cross when He agonized in sacrificial love. His body was stretched naked and uncovered to the world, His followers, and His mockers, that day on Calvary. Perhaps it is a statement about and to the body of Christ today. Exposed in sacrifice is exposed in love. Like Jesus, we must choose to die this death.

Sin had brought man and God to such a place of suffering, and yet, in that place, their covenant was again established, for at the cross love was shed. The Son of God and sons of men now had experienced crying and dying together, so we could emerge with the power to become sons and daughters of God. Eternity in heaven was released at the cross. Because heaven and hell are at the cross, at the crossroads of Calvary a decision of destiny must be made. Heaven and hell met at the cross—the heaven of God's love—And the hell of our sin--Love won a stunning victory. Will you choose heaven or hell?

CHAPTER TEN

Remember Me

> And one of the malefactors which were hanged railed on Him, saying, If thou be the Christ, save thyself and us. But the other answering rebuked him, saying, Dost not thou fear God, seeing thou art in the same condemnation? And we indeed justly; for we receive the due reward of our deeds; but this man hath done nothing amiss. And he said unto Jesus, Lord, <u>remember me</u> when thou comest into thy kingdom. And Jesus said unto him, Verily I say unto thee, Today shalt thou be with Me in paradise. Luke 23:39-43.

Man asks to be remembered to God.

Two men, condemned, alone, stripped and broken, hopeless, hungry, empty and without value to the world, are crucified next to Jesus. One man is angry at the punishment he bears, a just punishment for his deeds, and mocks the Son of God. This man has no repentance, he wants to be released from the penalty of his own sin. He says, "If you're the Son of God, come down, save yourself and us." The other says, "Remember me," and remembered he is, for Jesus replies, "Today, you will be with me in paradise."

This is because God doesn't look at the outward appearance. He looks at the heart. He doesn't look to a person's wealth, intelligence, gifts or goods, or any other thing that is important to this world. All those things are from Him and created by Him, and have no value disconnected from Him anyway. God's love is not dependent upon who we are. Jesus loved the sick, the lepers, the outcast, and the dead. God is love, and can do nothing else. Love depends on the heart of the giver. We cannot add anything to God's love, anymore than we can add to God.

So, Jesus gives the gift of eternal life to the man on the other cross. What does it profit a man to gain the whole world, but lose his soul? The whole world cannot buy eternal life. The thief had nothing left but to receive from God. He surely had nothing to give. He had no life to give. He had nothing to receive but eternity, and paradise it would be that day.

In the end we have nothing to give either, not money, fame, looks or name, not good works, positions, power or authority, but only to yield and receive. For the thief there was nothing left to barter with. No earthly transactions. He was a debtor to the world; he had been found wanting, and he was to pay with his life. The law condemned him to death that day. He was a debtor to God; he was a sinner. But at his execution, he gains eternity. All we will ever have is what the Son of Man bestows upon us by His grace and His working in us. We are all found wanting at the cross.

Here's what happened: God remembered the human race, condemned to die, by sending His Son to die alongside. And not only that, Jesus took on the condemnation of the man declared worthless to the world. This is our true state, debtors, condemned, and facing execution. God knows it and lets that be seen to the world; we take nothing into this world, and we certainly will take nothing out. The cross is the display case. We can see and the whole world can see our innermost being. At the three crosses, God displays our true state, and the true heart of God. Jesus and eternity hang in the balance—which is your cross?

Reality: We are condemned, stripped, alone, naked, and lost for eternity. In this story, one man acknowledges his state, and the other refuses to do so, or acknowledge God. This is a lesson revealed in scripture. As "sons of man" we have two crosses to choose from: One, the cross to paradise in recognition of sins, or two, the cross of judgment in denial. In one choice we return to the paradise of God and ultimately the tree of life, and at the other the last throes of the old nature having chosen the tree of the knowledge of good and evil, exits to eternity without God. We will die at one tree or the other.

In the center cross is the Son of God. It merges the tree of life and the tree of the knowledge of good and evil, into the tree of God. It is His cross, as sons and daughters of God we must choose as the path of life. In fact, God chooses this cross for His Son and all of His sons and daughters. No denial, no escape.

In this stripped down finality, we ask to be remembered to God, and God remembers us. Remember me, the thief says. Remember me, the lost, hopeless, and dying say. Remember me, we cry in our solitude and pain and fear. Remember your creation. The ultimate act of love and acknowledgement of the worth of His creation merges with the ultimate act of condemnation and rejection under the legal judgment for our deeds--that we might not be judged, but found righteous, and given access to eternal life by Jesus Christ.

Now the other thief represents another heart, rejecting the love of God, rejecting the sentence of the law, and rejecting the demands of God and man. God must have been thinking: Will man ever stop making up his own rules? Will they ever get the nature of love? Even at the cross where he is nailed without exit, this man will not accept the cross. It can't get any clearer. Yet, he denies the cross and the Man at the next cross. And here is a revelation of the heart of man again: Rebellious, making his own rules, rejecting the law of God and man, and rejecting the path of salvation. This man will experience the cross without correction, and without paradise. He is lost, but denies his lostness. Even at the point of death and judgment with no exit, he curses God. The book of Revelation describes such a man under judgment: "And the rest of the men which were not killed by these plagues yet repented not of the works of their hands, that they should not worship devils, and idols of gold, and silver, and brass, and stone, and of wood: which neither can see, nor hear, nor walk: Neither repented they of their murders, nor of their sorceries, nor of their fornication, nor of their thefts." Revelation 9:20-21.

Two representations of the heart of man. One angry and hard, the other humbly cries, Remember me. Jesus says, "Today you shall be with Me in paradise." And so God hears the cry, as His creation says, Remember me.

God asks to be remembered to Man.

> And He said unto them, With desire I have desired to eat this Passover with you before I suffer. For I say unto you, I will not any more eat thereof, until it be fulfilled in the kingdom of God. And He took the cup, and gave thanks, and said, Take this, and divide it among yourselves: For I say unto you, I will not drink of the fruit of the vine, until the kingdom of God shall come. And He took bread, and gave thanks, and brake it, and gave unto them, saying. This is My body which is given for you: this do in remembrance of Me. Likewise also the cup after supper, saying, This cup is the new testament of My blood, which is shed for you. Luke 22:15-20.

God asks to remembered to man. When all is said and done, peace is made between heaven and earth, God and man at the cross— peace on earth and good will to all men. In eating and sharing the Passover meal with His disciples, Jesus says, "Remember Me." For in this broken bread and cup of suffering, He tells us, I want you to remember forever what will take place in just a few hours from now when I am crucified. Remember Me and My sacrifice. Remember all that will be done. Remember all that you will attain with the new covenant that is written, secured, and sealed with My blood. Remember my suffering, and remember your God and what He has performed for you for now and eternity every time you touch this bread and wine in remembrance of Me.

We know that in this first Passover/communion, the bread represented the lamb killed and eaten which was to give strength to the body of His people, the children of Israel, as they passed over from the land of Egypt and bondage, to promise and freedom. The cup of wine corresponds to the blood of the lamb place on the lintels of each house so the angel of death would pass over in judgment. In many details, which I will not go into here, the Passover is a type of the cross where the Lamb of God was slain, His body broken, and blood spilled. Because of His sacrifice the angel of eternal death will pass over all who put themselves under the protection of that blood.

Jesus says, remember what was done at the cross, just as the children of Israel remembered the great deliverance of their God.

Remember Me. By My blood you are brought out of the bondage to sin and death to freedom and life in God. The blood of Jesus pays the price of a human life. You were never meant to be slaves, to sin or slaves to each other or any of the elements of this world. Gold and silver and currency and goods cannot buy a human soul. But more than that, only the blood of the Son of God can purchase sons and daughters of God who were made in the image and likeness of God, containers of His glory, and deliverers of His authority. This blood cleanses us from our iniquities—our sins, brokenness, moral illness, condemnation, guilt, and shame, so we can stand righteous before God, and come boldly to the throne of grace.

Remember Me. My blood gives you authority over all the power of Satan. Jesus spoiled, defeated, put down, all principalities and powers, rulers of the darkness of this world, spiritual wickedness in high places, localized demons, idols, curses, hexes, vexes, spells, incantations, psychic power, demonic prayers, and any other being or expression of the enemy. We have that same authority over evil forces and their kingdoms, to establish in His name, His kingdom, for His power and His glory, for we know that through the cross, He "spoiled principalities and powers, making an open show of them, triumphing over them in it." Colossians 2:15. This is through the power of the blood which cleanses us from sin and gives us the power of the crucified One. The blood reestablishes us as sons and daughters of God, with the authority that Jesus Himself left us.

Remember Me. You are more than a conqueror. That blood makes you pure, so the enemy has no access to your spirit. You may wear My righteousness as a breastplate, to keep you from mortal wounds of the enemy. Your righteous walk will keep you in integrity, and preserve you. Your obedience will guide your steps. You may hide in the secret place of the Most High, under the shadow of the

Almighty. Jesus said, "The prince of this world has nothing in Me." By the cleansing of the blood, and breaking of demonic strongholds in our lives, the access of the enemy is diminished, so he (Satan) has nothing in us to gain access and destroy our souls.

Remember Me. The shed blood of Jesus is mighty because it forgives and erases sin, and therein has been the problem of the human race, for sin gave access to demons, curses, bondage, corruption and death.

Remember Me. Your reconciliation is costing the blood of the Son of God; Who left His throne in heaven with a crown of glory, to wear a crown of thorns; Who left the honor of heaven to experience the ultimate shame; Who came from heaven to earth to the grave and Hades to break the bonds of death; Who allowed Himself to be reduced from the dimensions of God to the dimension of a man for this act of love; and Who knew no sin, yet became sin for the human race, past and present and future, causing the very earth to quake and darkness to cover the face of the sun.

Remember Me. My broken body has all the healing you need, for the restoration of heart, mind and soul. As we partake of His brokenness we take part of Jesus into us to experience His restorative and resurrection life.

> Surely he hath borne our grief and carried our sorrows: yet we did esteem him stricken, smitten of God, and afflicted. But he was wounded for our transgressions, he was bruised for our iniquities: the chastisement of our peace was upon him; and with his stripes we are healed...and the Lord hath laid on him the iniquity of us all. Isaiah 53:4-6.

Remember Me. As I hung on that tree, I bore the curse of the law. Remember that these curses are the generational penalties and patterns under the law that you have reaped from generation to generation for sins. By My cross, these generational curses and disposition to sin can be broken, and the traumas you experienced and the generations before you, so that you not only have forgiveness of your own sins, but can be freed of the bondage and oppression into which you were born. As I hung on that tree, I bore the iniquities of all, and the hurt and pain of all generations. Written in my blood in the heavenly realm was, "Forgive us *our* debts, as we forgive *our* debtors." "It is finished." All scores are settled. As the iniquities of the fathers are visited on the children to the third and fourth generation, that network of sin and bondage, shame, trauma, moral illness, loss, deprivation, condemnation and compulsion under which you labor can be absorbed and eradicated. Remember this portion of redemption.

Remember Me. As you partake of communion those broken bits are emblems of the broken life of God, they are seeds of life fed into your soul.

Remember Me. "For God so loved the world that He gave His only begotten Son, that whosoever believeth on Him should not perish but have everlasting life." John 3:16.

Remember Me. Just as that lamb of the Passover was killed, drained of blood, and eaten, the Son of God suffered greatly to break the power of sin, death, Satan and self. An extravagant and awesome price was paid.

Remember Me. Take your eyes off yourself. Your redemption draweth nigh. God loves you. Look to Him.

Remember Me. There is the potential for peace between God and man and woman. He has done all He must do to restore us to our rightful place as sons and daughters of God.

Remember Me. Jesus reverses all failure, death, destruction, futility, inability, shame, sin, sickness, bondage at the cross.

Remember Me. "There is none other name under heaven given among men whereby we must be saved." Acts 4:12.

Remember Me. It was His death for your life.

Remember Me.

CHAPTER ELEVEN

The Ultimate Servant:
He Carried the Weights of the Entire
Human Race

> You know that the rulers of the Gentiles lord it over
> them, and those who are great exercise authority
> over them. Yet it shall not be so among you; but
> whoever desires to become great among you, let
> him be your servant. And whoever desires to be first
> among you, let him be your slave—just as the Son of
> Man did not come to be served but to serve, and to
> give His life a ransom for many. Matthew 20:25-28.

He carried the burdens of the lowest of men on the cross after He
labored with that same instrument of destruction on His back
like a criminal, naked and alone through the streets of Jerusalem. In
a way He was a criminal, for He was crucified for being Himself,
"Jesus of Nazareth, King of the Jews," something unrecognizable to
the present world order. He broke the law of sin and death that ruled
over this world and the hearts of men and women. But He did it by
being a servant. Can anyone say He "lords" it over us?

Because Jesus released all the He was and owned, He was free
to carry the greatest burden of all, that which He never had to carry
of Himself: Sin and death, sickness and sorrow, bondage and moral
corruption. Paul writes:

> (He) made Himself of no reputation, and took upon
> Him the form of a servant, and was made in the
> likeness of men... He humbled Himself, and became
> obedient unto death, even the death of the cross.
> Philippians 2:7-8.

Then as a servant unto death He carried the petty sins, the sarcastic glances, perverted gestures, the immature attitudes of fallen men, women and children and their sick behavior; the child abusers, and the hypocrites, swindlers, murderers, addicts, and hate-mongers. He carried self-pity and crying binges and depression. He carried the anger and shame to which we are born, and the tiny selfish acts and intentional passivity that largely go unnoticed. Can you imagine that the Lord of Glory came from heaven and did this out of love? He hung in the middle of time, between heaven and earth, on behalf of heaven on earth, to absorb the ever widening pool of sin and its effect that continues to burden the planet. He defies time and the control of time. He carried our illness, mental, moral and physical, through the stripes on His tattered back.

By His complete submission, no one had control over Jesus. Men hire servants, or make slaves of others, because they do not want to carry their own burdens. He volunteered for the job without pay. He did the job under the control of nothing but the will of the Father and the power of the Holy Spirit. He was not recruited by human counsel; He was recruited in the counsels of heaven from the foundation of the world. His utter submission was to the Father, and the guidance of the Spirit, not to man. The result was to serve God and man as only the Son of God and the Son of Man could. Sure, they beat Him, spit on Him, crucified Him and buried Him, but He allowed it. Sin's nature and Satan's designs cast them into this prophetic role. Notice they did not raise Him from the dead—they couldn't do that—that part of the prophecy was saved for God.

He knew the cost in advance. The price is too high for anyone to pay anyway, for,

> (we) are not redeemed with corruptible things, like
> silver or gold, for your aimless conduct received by

> tradition from your fathers, but with the precious
> blood of Christ, as of a lamb without blemish and
> without spot. I Peter 1:18-19 (NKJV).

The Son of God cannot be bought or betrayed, as Judas found with his dirty money, and sons and daughters of God cannot be redeemed by money, only by blood. Slaves are bought by money, and servants are paid in money, but God didn't want slaves or servants; the price of redemption would no longer be sufficient in silver. He wanted children. He wanted a new creation generated from the seed of His Son planted in the earth and resurrected unto power. God had never forgotten His original intent or plan to make man and woman in His image and likeness.

He took those weights of the entire human race on Him so we would be able to carry His glory in us, an exceeding and eternal weight of glory. II Corinthians 4:17. As long as we carry the weights, the glory cannot come. We have a choice to carry the shame or the glory. He could have been selfish by the world's standards and simply carried the glory, and we can be selfish by God's standards in stubborn rebellion and continue to carry our sin and shame. It is the odd reversal of love. Sin and its defilement, the brokenness, demonic occupancy and curses, are not conducive to His presence. So He goes to the cross to show us how to shovel out the madness by our new authority in Him. He carries the guilt and shame, and pardons the sins. He breaks the curses there and erases the marks of this world. Now, He says, you are new today, and every day you will be newer. Apply what I have done in your life daily. Do not let My sacrifice lie dormant, apply My blood, you are a child of God, but you are also "becoming" one. Now you can be free to worship Me in spirit and in truth and be what you were designed to be, a container of My glory, a child of God, a tabernacle of the Living God, just as I tabernacled with you. You were created in My image and likeness, learn and grow to be like Me. All that I am and have is yours to share.

By giving us Himself, He also frees us from vain pursuits that waste our lives and deplete our eternal inheritance.

(H)ow much more shall the blood of Christ, who
through the eternal Spirit offered Himself without spot
to God, cleanse your conscience from dead works
to serve the Living God. Hebrews 9:13-14.

He became a servant of man to carry the weights of the whole world, so we could be sons and daughters of God to carry the weight of His glory. He traded His life for our death, so we could live His life and carry His person to the world. He reversed our destiny of eternal shame and damnation, so we could receive His eternal inheritance ruling and reigning with Him in this life and forever.

CHAPTER TWELVE

For God So Loved the World
A Missing Rib and a Bride Returns to
Her Maker

God was empty without someone to love, for God is love, and His character forbids this vacuum. He created a universe to release in perfect unity a creation that would reflect and circulate His love. God would be seen, loved, and worshipped everywhere. His creation would be loved in unique design, special capacity, and by its very existence. For what God has touched, is it not a display of love? In the highest order He created man and woman, a creation that could respond in like capacity to the love He had bestowed. He gave everything to man in paradise to demonstrate His love, even a helpmate, a companion of like spirit, soul and body. As Adam slept, his rib was removed, so Eve was created out of the flesh of Adam. We know this is a portrait of our Lord. Likewise, the new creation and bride born through His side at the cross is not created from the dust like Adam, but by the body and blood of Jesus Christ. Man and woman fellowshipped with God, covered in glory, basking in radiant wholeness and completion and love with their Creator, a reflection of His divinity.

When Adam and Even rejected that love in rebellion, God Himself was willing to die the God-kind of death to gain that love back. On the cross Jesus was pierced in His side to show the world in the flesh the empty place of the eternal Husband longing for His bride, the eternal Father God longing to be filled again with the love of His highest creation, the eternal Spirit longing to nurture, recreate and restore.

He illustrates that without love we are forced to die. The hole in His heart was in the spirit before it was in the flesh. God was vulnerable to the uttermost. If God does not hide, should we? The emptying of God had been ordained from the foundation of the world because God's love never fails. The missing rib was to be put back in the side of the Second Adam for creation to be recreated, this time not in the flesh but in the spirit. The First Adam gives birth to a bride in the flesh. The Second Adam gives birth to a bride in the spirit, the whole race. He calls us to come back to the Creator, be born again in His side by water and blood. Let's try again—our marriage, our unity, to bear fruit for eternity. God was putting the rib back so we could be like our Creator, with His nature, His blood, His life, His wholeness, of same flesh, blood and Spirit. A missing rib, and a bride returns to her Maker's side to be recreated, and the Creator and creation are released to give and receive love. In the grave He slept in death until the work was complete and His bride could emerge from His side.

What was lost in the fall was so much—man and woman lost their capacity to love. The circles of love became smaller and smaller. With rebellion and disobedience against God, in fact, we lost our ability to even love ourselves. Selfishness became a perverted kind of self-love. Actually, it was self-hate masquerading as self-love for it enhanced separation and secretly proclaimed that death had triumphed over life. It was the creature despising the image that God the Giver destined within. It was not the love of self that the Father desired from which wholeness, community and responsibility could flow through the power and glory of God. And so, humankind floated away in its own darkness. God could have let us go, but even as we floated in sullenness and self-will, we were anchored by a thread, the scarlet thread that runs through the ages, the blood atonement. God had never let go. He always wanted reconciliation of that love relationship. His heart remained empty for His sons, daughters, wife. So, just as He had done the work to create us, He did the work to draw us back with cords of love and recreate us in His image.

The loving Father waits at the steps of His house to watch in the distance for the prodigal son. He does not enjoy the luxury of His house without His son.

The loving Husband hangs on a cross to validate His love and enable His betrothed wife to love back. He allows her to change there the dirty garments of disobedience at a place where He will bear the shame, not her, and put on a new gown without spot, wrinkle, blemish, or any such thing. He will take on Himself the dirtiness. He faithfully fulfills the role of the ultimate Husband for His bride by the washing of the water of the (W)ord at the cross. There He takes the responsibility of reconciliation for her unfaithfulness, even though He is not to blame.

The new bride would not come from the perfect, but the ranks of the worn out woman at the well, the Gadarene demoniac, the lepers, the woman with the issue of blood, doubtful paralytic at the pool of Bethesda, faithless disciples and the faithful Mary Magdalene who meets her Lord and Bridegroom in a cemetery, fresh from the grave. God so loved the world. The bride is a heavenly creation.

The loving Holy Spirit sings, declares, decrees, and pleads throughout the earth to call back the lost ones engaged in vain pursuits and other lovers.

God is a jealous God. His name is Jealous. Exodus 34:14. This is not the jealousy of earthly insecurity or even true betrayal (though in betrayal we experience what He has), but the bond of everlasting commitment and unequaled love, expansive provision, and supernatural protection. It is to secure in His creation's participation in the divine nature as originally intended. It requires covering and covenant, fusion into His life and body. Jesus bought us back with His own blood. If we miss Him, we will miss the entire plan of God. The Father, Son and Holy Spirit have poured all into creation and salvation and restoration. The Godhead is jealous to protect all that.

Jesus came on earth from the bosom, the heart, of the Father, and the Father opens wide a space for Jesus to return, but not alone. Jesus allows Himself be disassembled and recreated just for us, for Jesus let His whole body die on the cross, so His body could be whole, so a hole in His heart could be filled. The Holy Spirit waits in anticipation to fill the emptiness, the hole, in our hearts that was caused when we left God, and comes to resurrect in us the face of Jesus Christ as we ask Jesus in, giving true identity to a creature without one. And then the end is as the beginning, an eternal life of fellowship, covered by His glory, and basking in radiant wholeness, completion and love with the Creator.

CHAPTER THIRTEEN

Peace on Earth, Good Will Toward Men

Then the soldiers of the governor took Jesus into the common hall, and gathered unto Him the whole band of soldiers. And they stripped Him, and put on Him a scarlet robe. And when they had platted a crown of thorns, they put it upon His head, and a reed in His right hand: and they bowed the knee before Him, and mocked Him, saying, Hail, King of the Jews! And they spit upon Him and took the reed and smote Him on the head. And after that they had mocked Him, they took the robe off from Him, and put His own raiment on Him, and led Him away to crucify Him. And as they came out, they found a man of Cyrene, Simon, by name: him they compelled to bear His cross. And when they were come unto a place called Golgotha, that is to say, a place of a skull, they gave Him vinegar to drink mingled with gall: and when He had tasted thereof, He would not drink. And they crucified Him, and parted His garments, casting lots: that it might be fulfilled that which was spoken by the prophet, they parted my garment among them, and upon my vesture did they cast lots. And sitting down they watched Him there; and set up over His head His accusation written: THIS IS JESUS THE KING OF THE JEWS. Matthew 27:27-37.

In the book of Revelation the Lord Jesus Christ comes back to the earth on a white horse and rescues the world from its madness. And finally, at last, there will be peace on earth. The people of His time dreamed of such a Messiah to overthrow the yoke of the Roman Empire, but ultimately rejected Him because He did not match their expectation, lowly and sitting on a donkey, urging them to repent and love one another.

Yet, the bloody beachhead of the final invasion of Revelation was waged long ago in the war's greatest battle in the dirt and dust of Calvary. It was waged then by the one sacrificial warrior and Lamb, Son and humble man. The armies of heaven were not present. The rescue of earth was through the blood shed by the Lord of Hosts. In the book of Revelation, He is revealed again in kingly authority, and glory shines from the radiant Son of God. His eyes are a flame of fire, His vesture is dipped in blood. He is crowned with many crowns. He is KING OF KINGS AND LORD OF LORDS, Faithful and True, the Word of God. He is followed by the host of the redeemed and mighty angels.

> [13]And he *was* clothed with a vesture dipped in blood: and his name is called The Word of God. [14]And the armies *which were* in heaven followed him upon white horses, clothed in fine linen, white and clean. [15]He will smite the nations and rule them with a rod of iron, treading the winepress of the fierceness and wrath of God. Revelation 19.

But this was preceded by the crown of thorns and the blood of the cross where He had no vesture to soak the blood. There He died alone, His body in tatters, Satan's forces seeming to win.

His body streamed with the blood that would be the blood of love, the life-love pressed out of Him to create the wine of the new covenant, willingly offered to the winepress of God's judgment and man's wrath, for all who repent and believe.   The Father had substituted His judgment on an unruly and rebellious world to His innocent Son. When God's judgment finally does come, it will be the Lamb who is able to open the seals of judgment, because He took our judgment on earth, an offer which has largely been rejected.

God gave a second chance through His Son to mediate peace. Violence was done to Him, so His children could take back His kingdom, for the violent take the kingdom of heaven by force. Because of this battle someday He will come back on a white horse to topple the kingdoms of this world and their counterfeit gods.

When the angels declared peace on earth, good will to all men, at His birth, the joyous listeners did not understand what peace would cost. There was a battleground of peace on earth—peace by the blood of the cross, where Jesus, the Mediator of the new covenant, mediates with His own life. We are washed with His blood so we may once again be grafted into relationship with the Father and receive His blessing, inheritance and love. We are also established in holiness and righteousness to come into a proper love relationship with others.

> For this is the message that you have heard from the beginning, that you should love one another, not as Cain who was of that wicked one, and slew his brother. And wherefore slew he him? Because his own works were evil and his brother's righteous. I John 3:11-12.

We are healed and strengthened by His body as part of the new covenant abiding with His wholeness and life, for His cross exists for the healing of His people, a tree of life.

> And having made peace through the blood of His cross, by Him to reconcile all things unto Himself; by Him, I say, whether they be things in earth, or things in heaven. And you that were sometime alienated and enemies in your mind by wicked works, yet now hath He reconciled in the body of His flesh through

death, to present you holy and unblamable and unreproveable in His sight. Colossians 1:20-22.

The aliens were no longer alien, they became children of God. We could be released from our wicked works by the cross. There would be no final victory in the war had not the battle of the cross been won. Battles of the cross continue today.

Sadly, this peace is disregarded, disputed and denied by many, for to share this peace you must partake of the life-giving blood and body. You must stay at the cross and die there yourself, to be revived in resurrection power in this life and in the world to come. All warriors, sons, daughters, servants, friends, and the bride of Jesus Christ will be found there. It is the gate to the city of God, and outside that gate will be all sorcerers, the immoral, murderers, idolaters, those who love to lie, and others who will not inherit the kingdom. Your blood is worthless to take you to eternity. It is corruptible. Only He has the power of an endless life.

Paul writes:

> That at that time you were without Christ, being aliens from the commonwealth of Israel and strangers from the covenants of promise, having no hope, and without God in the world: But now in Christ Jesus you who sometimes were far off are made nigh by the blood of Christ. For He is our peace, who hath made both one, and hath broken down the middle wall of partition between us: having abolished in His flesh the enmity, even the law of commandments contained in ordinances; for to make in Himself of twain, one new man, so making peace; And that He might reconcile both unto God in one body by the cross, having slain the enmity thereby: And came and preached peace to you which were afar off, and to them that were nigh, for through Him we both have access by one Spirit unto the Father. Ephesians 2:12-18.

He reconciles Jew and Gentile, strangers and sons. He abolishes the law of the commandments separating Jew and Gentile from each other to remake both in the image of God, capable of fulfilling the law of love whereby hostilities between God and all of us, and all peoples, races, and tongues will cease. He breaks down divisions in society, physically, economically, and spiritually, for there is neither Jew nor Gentile, male nor female, bond nor free—we are all one in the body of Christ, and there, peace should rule, for Christ is not divided. We submit to Him and each other.

Some day when the church, the body of Christ, is purified to obedience and holiness, it will raise to its rightful place of unity and power at His side, as any bride. Jesus does not divide as the world divides, He divides as the Word divides, clean from unclean, darkness from light, holy from unholy, soul from spirit.

However, there were and are alternative methods to peace at any cost, a peace at the utmost cost. From God's point of view, God could have eliminated us completely and the earth would have returned to its primal, empty state, overrun by demonic outlaws. This almost happened with the flood, except God had a plan working through righteous Noah. There could be peace with total annihilation, but it would be a desolate one because God is a God of fullness and life and creativity. Even though judgment may have called for this solution, such a peace was not His highest desire.

Instead, He decided upon the solution of love expressed in the lives of His people in their obedience and sacrifices, all portraits and symbols before Jesus Christ. For peace to exist between God and His creation and between men, either we die or God dies. At the cross both will die, so the exchange can be made. The old sinful nature of men and women has to die, so the rebellion and disobedience could be put to death; and Jesus, the Son of God, had to die to enable this by bearing our sins, iniquities, grief, sorrows, condemnation, sicknesses and death on the cross. God had a right to righteous judgment but He released this on His Son, so we could live up to Jesus' righteousness. Any peace that does not deal with the conflict in our souls will always be a false peace, an insecure peace, and a temporary peace. As James writes:

Where do wars and fights come from among you?

> Do they not come from your desires for pleasure that
> war in your members? You lust and do not have.
> You murder and covet and cannot obtain. You fight
> and war. Yet you do not have because you do not
> ask. James 4:1-2 (NKJV).

At the same time there has always been a counterfeit vision of peace, and this is peace from the unregenerate human viewpoint. There is peace by control and force and false plans of unity. These have one major common denominator: There is peace through ungodly standardization of life, stripping humanity of its potential participation in the divine nature through Jesus Christ, so we all may be equally lost without true identity and eternal hope. This is peace without freedom, "Pax Romana," the Third Reich, dictatorships, and other totalitarian regimes—all have this element in common to a greater or lesser extent. Such killing coercion is embedded in "free" societies as well that squeeze the way, truth, and life of God out of the community, for only where the Spirit of the Lord is, is there true liberty.

So Jesus was killed by the law of the Romans for declaring He was the King of the Jews, a treasonous act. Roman law had to be administered no matter how unwillingly Pontius Pilate executed it. Similarly, He was killed by the Jews through the Romans because He declared He was their Messiah, the King of the Jews, and Son of God, a blasphemous act, for they refused His authority. The Jews killed their own promise of a Messiah, preferring to misapply their own law and remain willingly blind to their prophets, thereby denying this promise for one main reason: Had they accepted Him, they would be truly ruled by submission of their hearts. Obedience to man was preferable than obedience to God whereby their control would be dissolved, even if it could have released them from bondage.

You cannot control true leaders, so people in power, will want to discredit or discard them. Likewise, people who open their hearts to the King are potentially a threat. Governments large and small, demonic and human, will always try to strip away the anointing of the Holy Spirit, and the divine nature of individuals rooted in their knowledge and love of the Jesus Christ, for they put at risk those kingdoms.

Peace on earth by killing God has been man's plan and the enemy's plan for awhile. It was the design of Satan in the garden, and it was the design of the Pharisees and sinners and Romans and all of us to stabilize and justify our lives by eliminating the conditions of God which serve to demonstrate our sin and incompleteness without Him. This plan gained its ultimate expression (to date) when Jesus came to earth culminating in His false trial and crucifixion. But the plan backfired according to God's redemptive purpose and glory. This plan will rear its ugly head again when Antichrist comes, as the world celebrates its humanistic unfaithfulness to its Creator in the worship of self and the final worship of the one exalting himself above the knowledge of God.

Jesus said He did not come to bring peace, but to bring a sword. He has been and always will be the divider, the sifter of our souls. From the human point of view, the solution is to eliminate God— Take Him to the cross again and leave Him there, for many do not want His division and the painful convicting power of His love. The world prefers the accusations of the enemy to the conviction of the Holy Spirit. Jesus said, the Holy Spirit comes to reprove the world of sin, righteousness and judgement.

> Of sin, because they believe not on Me; Of righteousness because I go to My Father and ye see Me no more; of judgment, because the prince of this world is judged. John 16:8-11

The world does not want to be corrected. Therefore, the next best solution is to eliminate the knowledge of God in the earth realm and the body of Christ in whom the indwelling Holy Spirit lives.

In the book of Revelation this false plan of peace originating from the prince of this world, will be hell on earth, reflective of its source. (Is not hell the total absence of God? They wanted a world without God. Instead they got a world without Christ under God's direct judgment.) Nevertheless, the prince of this world has already been judged and despite his death maneuvers, is just awaiting the final execution of his sentence. Satan has lost, but in his delusion, he believes he can win. Accordingly, the plan will fail.

Jesus comes to us in this dispensation as the Lamb of God that takes away the sin of the world. By doing so He absorbs that element of human life, sin, that brings disunity and strife, and therefore, wars and division in our souls and to our neighbors and with our God. We know that the cross has two bars, the vertical one symbolizing Jesus' relationship and obedience to God and the horizontal bar indicating the Lord's outstretched love to us. He demonstrated the great commandment to utter completion pouring out His love in both directions. So, with extended arms and divine obedience, Jesus the Mediator of the new covenant and our peace calls each individual to join Him at the foot of the cross, put down his weapons and banners, and take up his cross daily and follow Him. He died at His cross, so we could also die there and take up our crosses daily.

He urges us to come to Him now in utmost love, just as the Father waits in anticipation looking for sons and daughters to enter through the gates of heaven, and the Holy Spirit woos us in spirit and in truth. Someday the door of the cross will be shut, and earth will meet her Maker riding on a white horse with eyes aflame of fire.

CHAPTER FOURTEEN

The Tree of Life

There were two trees in the middle of the garden of God, the tree of life, and the tree of the knowledge of good and evil. Of these the Scripture states:

> The Lord God planted a garden eastward in Eden and there He put the man whom He had formed. And out of the ground the Lord God made every tree grow that is pleasant to the sight and good for food. The tree of life was also in the midst of the garden, and the tree of the knowledge of good and evil.... And the Lord God commanded the man saying, "Of every tree of the garden you may freely eat: but of the tree of the knowledge of good and evil you shall not eat, for in the day that you eat of it you shall surely die." Genesis 2: 8-9, 16-17.

Of the tree of the knowledge of good and evil, every person on the planet will taste, and of the tree of life some will eat. These trees represent all our lives.

The Word of God often likens people and nations to trees and the two trees in the Garden of Eden can describe the personality and history of all of us. They are incorporated into the life of each man and woman who either chooses to serve God, or serve self under the power and seduction of Satan. Every tree and every life begins with a seed. Life will be determined by the type of seed which is planted, and the soil, moisture, fertilization, and the "light" to which it is exposed. The pressure and circumstances of the environment of the seed   will cause that seed to release its roots downward and shoots upward. There is a visible and an invisible realm to all living things. We can see the trunk, branches, leaves and fruit of the tree, but we cannot see the original seed, the root system, the entire soil of growth, or the internal fluids which bring it life. In fact we cannot see "life" we can only see its evidence of its existence. God compares us to trees. We can easily understand the nature of a tree.

God created two trees in the middle of the Garden of Eden. The life of the sinner with the old nature can be likened to the tree of the knowledge of good and evil, a tree of death masquerading as life. The desire for this tree are seeds of Satan, lies planted in the soil of the hearts of mankind. We are clearly told in the Genesis account what these lies were.

> Now the serpent was more subtle than any beast of the field which the Lord God had made. And he said unto the woman, Yea, hath God said, Ye shall not eat of every tree of the garden? And the woman said unto the serpent, We may eat of the fruit of the trees of the garden: But of the fruit of the tree which is in the midst of the garden, God hath said, Ye shall not eat of it, neither shall ye touch it, lest ye die. And the serpent said unto the woman, Ye shall not surely die: For God doth know that in the day ye eat thereof then your eyes shall be opened, and ye shall be as gods, knowing good and evil. And when the woman saw that the tree was good for food, and that it was pleasant to the eyes, and a tree to be desired to make one wise, she took of the fruit thereof, and did eat, and gave also unto her husband with her; and he did eat. Genesis 3:1-6.

These lies Satan sowed in the heart of Eve perverted the authority of God's word. As a result, Jesus Christ, the manifestation and image of God and the "Word of God" could no longer be reproduced in Adam and Eve. Man and woman became disfigured in line with the new "seed" of death, "self-godlikeness," which was planted within them. They changed in destiny from being in the image and likeness of the true and living God with the characteristics of eternal love and life, to being their own little "gods" mimicking what they could have been. They became creatures of limited time and understanding, corrupted with a spiritual virus called sin, and perishing by the minute.

Furthermore, God had to take eternal life away from them by barring them from the tree of life. To allow their counterfeit version of life to continue eternally would be a denial of His truth and being, contaminating the universe. The lies Satan sowed perverted man and woman's relationship to God, designed to be the highest creation living in obedience to God and with God-given authority over the earth. These lies also perverted our true nature distorting our purpose from serving God to serving self, and determining our own destiny, which was naturally limited, instead of a God-given destiny. These lies continue to be planted in the world today by the father of lies, the devil. It is only through Jesus, who planted eternity again in our hearts, that we could have a destiny in the image and likeness of God.

In the Garden, eternal life was stripped from Adam and Eve. The slippage of the foundation from God to self brought an earthquake in the spirit, and the death of spiritual life brought death to the realm of the soul and body for Adam and Eve. Without a relationship with God, or a severed and insecure relationship, the steps of a disobedient man were not ordered. They were lame and perverted and they went away from the paths we were to dwell in, the paths of righteousness. Continued sin was inevitable. Not hearing from God, other voices and other influences crept in. Humanity's source changed from a limitless God to a limited self. The fruit of the tree from which humanity ate was the tree of the knowledge of good and evil. The Lord told His creation, "Do not eat of this tree of touch it lest you die." They touched it and they died. The vision of God was snatched from their eyes, and they were left incomplete, lame and blind, trying to live eternally, or with sad knowledge of an eternal dimension, without eternal life. Instead of life being a free-flowing river of love and joy in the presence of God, it became a forced march.

The tree of the knowledge of good and evil will always be in opposition to the tree of life. Knowledge of good and evil is limited to what humans think and feel, and whatever spiritual forces they tap into, and is founded on self-exaltation. It depends on what is known, controlled and discerned. It means making up one's own rules and doing what appeals to the sense and soul realm. It is becoming god-like with the exclusion of God. The ultimate expression of this is the man of sin, the Antichrist, revealed in the book of Revelation. The tree had all the limitations of human beings in the physical and soul realm and extended demonic knowledge in the spiritual realm. It was a tree of death masquerading as life. Through the fall, our foundation on the "Rock" was shattered, and humanity began its awful slide into superficiality that brings destruction with every shifting value.

God spoke out the end result of the disobedience with the curses described in Genesis Chapter 3. These are fundamental curses relating to the fallen man and woman's new experience of life and themselves, and woman's relationship to man—which are based on the removal of the covering, blessing and provision of God. Humanity's lifeline was no longer connected to God, but to the world, and what could be consumed in pursuit of self. Instead of being led by the Holy Spirit, evil spirits gained influence over God's prime creation. Man found himself in bondage to self, having to earn his way by the sweat of his brow. Woman found herself subject to man, for her desire would be for her husband and he would rule over her. Her life was identified with multiplied conception and sorrow. Both were in bondage to the law of sin and death. The glory cloud that had covered them had disappeared, and they would suffer the curse of living life without its designed eternal dimension in the glory of God. Man must work for himself, seek for himself and gain his own glory instead of being clothed in the glory of God. After the fall, Eve, too, lost the glory of God as her covering, and now needed the covering of the man. Their pitiful attempts to cover their shame, as the glory of God departed, finally required the death of animals, slain by the Father, to cover their bodies and, even more, their fallen state evidencing their disobedience. This secret shame would be reproduced in the lives of each person entering the planet for a new world order emerged when innocence was lost.

The curses in the garden did not end the curses for disobedience that fallen man and woman would experience. In the fullness of time, the Lord God gave the law to the children of Israel. The law defined obedience to God and the resulting blessings for obedience, and defined penalties and curses for disobedience. It was a simple system. The law, God's method of preserving life and a righteous nation to produce a righteous "Seed," was not known throughout the earth. The nations did not have the revelation of the Jews, but salvation is of the Jews. The Jewish people had the answer but did not share it as originally intended. However, all people still bore the weight and burden of condemnation, curses, and penalties without revelation. The world was already condemned when Jesus arrived on the scene. The curses of disobedience described in Deuteronomy 28, were no less applicable to the heathen nations as they were to the Jews. Sickness, poverty, family breakdown, fear, broken relationships between God and man and between men, wars, dissatisfaction, political domination, servitude, famine, and other curses were applicable, even if the nations did not know the law. If you sow to the flesh, you will of the flesh reap corruption. These sorrowful results of sin are the inheritance of the human race that denied Father God, and instead received an inheritance from the father of lies, Satan. The sin nature and the generational patterns and curses of sin held the world in bondage.

The Lord tells us in the Ten Commandments that the iniquities of our earthly fathers would be visited on the third and fourth generation for lawbreakers. Exodus 20:5. The word "iniquity" means evil, fault, sin, iniquity, guilt, blame, moral illness, perversion, crookedness; in short—the evil bent of our lives. We are quite simply, the fruit of our parents. In some ways we are all predisposed to be "morally ill" in certain areas and expressed in sin when the right opportunity presents itself. Because of this spiritual reality we bear the guilt and blame of people we do not even know, clouding our perceptions and weighing down our lives. David writes: "I was shapen in iniquity and in sin did my mother conceive me." Psalms 51:5. Clearly because of sin, curses of disobedience and patterns of disobedience are passed from generation to generation, creating in the soil of the sin nature, i.e. human nature born spiritually dead and predisposed to sin, confirmation of the above law spoken by the Lord in Exodus 20:5.

Furthermore, instead of being led of the Holy Spirit, evil spirits gained influence and access to God's prime creation. Satan, who was cursed to failure, became the god of this world. Under him ruled principalities, powers, rulers of the darkness of this world, spiritual wickedness in high places, satanic angels, and demonic localized hosts. There was a changing of the guard. Instead of man and woman exercising dominion through godly power and authority with God as their head, dispatching through creation heavenly hosts, Satan exercised dominion through his hierarchy controlling men and women.

These sadly "new" creatures were forbidden to touch the tree of life now, or sin would be eternally perpetuated in eternally destructive bodies. Humanity slowly waited until the Savior would die on the tree of life, the cross, to set them free from this cursed tree of death from which they had eaten to live more fully. Satan's great short-cut, fulfilling one's destiny without obedience to God, had reversed the essence of our existence; eternal beings can only reach fulfillment through nurture in the fertile soil of a heart in communion with God, receiving living waters, divine seeds of the word, and holy light from an eternal God.

The life of the sinner with the old nature can be likened to the tree of the knowledge of good and evil, a tree of death masquerading as life. The origin of this tree are seeds of Satan, the "unword", lies planted in the soil of the hearts of mankind. The root system is based on the iniquities and sins of the fathers which are passed on from generation to generation, and curses from disobedience, released on sinners and their descendants for violation of the law of God, and the unsanctified flesh of the "sons of Adam." As the tree begins to grow, the trunk may be compared to the "self" which bears the weight of the branches, and is the visible expression of the life from the roots. In most lives, the "self" does not know its origin, saying I am "such and such" a person, without knowledge of why they are bent in a particular way. But clearly we must look at the roots and consider the seed. Some of the branches growing from the stump appear evil, such as rebellion, pride, disobedience, witchcraft, etc., and some appear good, such as the pride of life, humanism, good works, worldly acceptance and success. However, all are counterfeit because their origin is not of God. Their shoots are the work of the flesh. The fruit is sin, which when eaten, incorporate the taste of more ungodly works; or having fallen to the ground, reproduce and export the same tree into the soil of other hearts. The seeds reproduce the same kind. The covering of the tree are its leaves, evil spirits, and a covering of false glory, but evil spirits also circulate through the root system and branches and give life to this corrupt tree. The tree has a false covering of the flesh and the works of the flesh, and their empty show. Lives based on the father of lies will grow in his image. Jesus wants to lay the axe of God to the roots of all such trees.

On the other hand, there is a transition between this tree of death and the tree of life through the blood of Jesus. The tree of death and the tree life merge with the cross. The seed God planted in the earth, Jesus Christ, grows in all who will receive Him to create the kingdom of heaven. However, the tree of death must be uprooted. While a beautiful tree of life could have been freely experienced in the Garden by Adam and Eve, now the tree becomes the cross. There Jesus again establishes in the earth realm the power to become sons and daughters of God, releasing to us eternal life. God knows we must die there to receive of this life. The tree in the middle of Mount Calvary is our tree of life, but it is a tree used for the vilest of purposes, it is stripped and broken and cursed. At the cross the tree of life merges with the tree of the knowledge of good and evil. The tree of the knowledge of good and evil was really an execution instrument to kill God and an instrument of destruction of our intended identity and potential in God. Stripped of its prettiness that is all it is.

Yes, that seductive tree of the knowledge of good and evil had its prettiness, it made one wise, and was good to the taste. Many people in this world experience the good side of the tree--personal power, wealth and position, choosing their own way, the pleasures of the flesh without God's boundaries and many joys of the world—perhaps the path of a religion or philosophy (or not), love and life and family they consider "good." Others simply experience their existence without the true God. But with that tree comes another terrifying reality, an inevitably real and terrifying side, whether we know it or not. We also get the knowledge of evil. God never intended us to know about death and dementia, abuse and cancer, rape, addiction, suicide, war and famine. What a horror to realize that the knowledge of evil accompanies the knowledge of good. Understand that the word "knowledge" in scripture includes intimacy with that condition. So what was the prize of this tree in reality? An intimate knowledge of death, sickness, sorrow, brokenness, and everything else under the law of sin and death. And even if life is considered "good" and "full" and "happy" as our Western minds and hearts tend to gravitate, eventually there will be eternal separation from God. Yes, Adam's seed got the knowledge of good and the knowledge of evil. Through one man, Adam, sin entered the human race. But at the cross God proved He is above good and bad, our versions of right and wrong, what we choose and what we don't, who's in and who's out and who's up and who's down. He is God. The first shall be last and the last shall be first. At the cross Jesus absorbed all the "knowledge" that we received of both good and evil of that false tree masquerading as the tree of life, everything that exalts itself above the knowledge of God, and replaces it with the true knowledge of God, who is only good and holy, true and righteous. At the cross Jesus absorbs both our definitions and experiences of good and evil and replaces them with a knowledge of Him: To know Him, the power of His resurrection, and the fellowship of His suffering. Philippians 3:10. He replaces temporary life, the magnification of time and self, with eternal life, the magnification of Him. And what is eternal life? John 17:3. This is life eternal, that they might know thee the only true God, and Jesus Christ, whom thou hast sent. At the cross, Jesus absorbs the end game of the tree of the knowledge of good and evil, and replaces it with the rugged, bloody tree of life He sacrificially accepts in His divine, sublime, incomparable leap of faith, hope and love.

The cross shows the ultimate reality of the tree of the knowledge of good and evil. Satan thought he was pulling off the same coup at the cross as he did in the Garden with the other tree. However, the Son of God used the reality of this tree of death and reverses its power by choosing to die there. In His redemptive love God also allows men the choice to die there and leave their counterfeit lives and god-likeness in the image of self at the foot of the cross, these forgeries being the satanic reversal of God's true creation of man and woman in God's image and likeness. Satan first steals our identity, devaluing us to be "as gods" in the likeness of all other men, but Jesus brings perfection back to our lives in the image of the one true God. Anyone who does not accept this work of Jesus, loses his soul, and therefore a chance to restore his divine identity in and through Jesus Christ.

As they were driven from the Garden, Cherubims guarded the tree of life with a flaming sword which turned every way, lest Adam and Eve eat of it and become immortal rebels. Adam and Eve would have to die to get to the tree of life. That is still the case, the seed of Adam must die to come to the tree of life at the cross.

The cross shows man and Satan's foolish attempt to make God in man's image and likeness, thereby making man and this earth ends in themselves and reversing God's great act of creation, the unlimited potential to become sons of God. Sinful men and women did not want the God they truly had. Had the satanic plan succeeded it would have proved the serpent's counterfeit that life could actually be lived "as gods," and that there is not one true God. But such a position was impossible to substantiate, for it was advanced by the father is lies, and therefore could not bear fruit, only emptiness.

Actually the Lie killed himself that day at the great showdown of the cross. The emptiness of the lie was demonstrated during the time of the law and the prophets by those who believed the promises of God. But that day Satan was finished and the kingdom of heaven established forever to be released and validated in our lives until He comes. Men like Pontius Pilate waver and say, "What is truth," not even comprehending the concept. But Truth sprang forth from the ground on resurrection day, thereby affirming Truth, by the power of Life, and demonstrating the Way.

Unlike the tree of the knowledge of good and evil, the cross did not have a sweet flavor when originally eaten by our Lord, for it was not "good to the taste," as was the fruit of the tree of the knowledge of good and evil. It was and is a bitter cup, but it yields the peaceable fruits of righteousness, the fruits of the Spirit, and the fruit of eternal life from which a lost world may eat. It was a sacrifice of a sweet savor to God, not men, who only see death. There we can truly taste and see the Lord is good. It was not "pleasant to the eyes," as the tempter's tree, for Jesus in the midst of that tree was not a beguiling, seductive presence like the serpent, but He was stripped, broken and cursed there, giving us a true view of the serpent's deadly effect on creation and his desired intention to kill God and the image of God in us. The light of the sun had to be blotted out that day because of the upheaval of nature at the death of the Son of God, and the separation of Father God from His own Son. Jesus "had no form or comeliness, and when we shall see Him, there is no beauty that we should desire Him." Isaiah 53:2. This tree was an executioner's instrument, and on it was the executed Son of God, who was killed in the hearts of Adam and Eve as soon as they ate that first fruit. No, it was not "pleasant to the eyes." But through it the glory of God would be revealed to our eyes. It did not exalt our wisdom, for it was not a tree "desired to make one wise," as was the tree of the knowledge of good and evil. The cross was and continues to be foolishness to the world; it defeats the wisdom of men. All must come to it humbly as children, and leave at the cross their own thoughts and programs and sins and attitudes and conditions and positions and lives. Yet it releases the love and wisdom and power and authority of Jesus Christ to all who receive its truth, love and power.

As we go to the cross in repentance, where the tree of the knowledge of good and evil merges with the tree of life, a transition occurs. A new nature is born of the Spirit of God, by the divine Seed, Jesus, planted in our hearts. The new tree that grows in us is rooted and grounded in love. It is saturated with the water of the Holy Spirit, and grows in increase with the Word of God. The trunk is the new person in Jesus Christ, where He increases and we decrease, for flesh, blood, and self must have no preeminence. Its main branches are love to God and love to man—the essence of the great commandment--with such smaller branches defining the same, such as obedience, hope, faith and holiness. Fruits of the Spirit and gifts of the Spirit reproduce the life of this tree in the hearts of others. By it the old nature, the curses of the law and sin are broken, for Jesus took upon Himself the curse of the law, becoming a curse for us. Galatians 3:13. He has the power of an endless life, returning eternity to us and enabling us to break free from the patterns of sin and self that perpetuate the limited, pitiful distance of our existence without Him. The Holy Spirit covers this tree and also circulates in the roots and branches. Its beautiful covering of leaves also are the covering of the believer, the beauty of holiness, garments of salvation, praise and righteousness. That which brings shame, He takes on the cross and gives us as our inheritance the garments of His glory, which He left behind in heaven. He takes our name and identity, as the Son of Man, so we may become sons and daughters of God. He takes our limitation and powerlessness and victimization, and gives us eternal authority and power and victory. He takes our sins and gives salvation. He takes our nothingness and feeble garments to cover that nothingness, and gives of His fullness, and robes of righteousness for of His fullness we have all received. He is full of grace and truth. He takes our evil inheritance from a lying spiritual father, and makes us joint-heirs with Him with our Heavenly Father.

Only the awesome love of God could conceive of such a plan— one from the foundation of the world. He clothes us totally in His life and in Him, so we may become His body with His blood circulating through our spiritual veins. The cross is a tree of life, because Jesus was obedient unto death. The believer is in transition from the first tree to the second tree through the cross. At the cross kingdoms of sin, Satan, sickness and self are stripped away so that we may become new creatures in Christ Jesus. By the cross the old nature and its fruits and roots are destroyed so new life can grow. And so we have the tree of life in our lives also.

Which tree will we become? "Come, everyone who thirsts, come to the waters; and you who have no money, come, buy and eat." Isaiah 55:1. "(T)he one who comes to Me, I will by no means cast out." John 6:37.

Paradise was made for man and woman. It was a human-centered place of abundant blessing. Heaven is God's dwelling place. It is

God-centered, a place of spiritual rulership, authority, blessing, love, creativity, and worship. Because man and woman wanted to be "as gods" by keeping their lives to themselves, and were not content to be as they were, created in the image and likeness of God, they actually are forced to be "like gods." Notice "gods", not "God," a multitude rather than unified with the One true God. They must leave paradise behind and enter an earth where, in one alternative, their daily choices will take them to an eternal destiny apart from God. The more separation, the more gods are formed, the more distance from the true image of God. The only other alternative is choosing truly to be "like God" by laying down their lives at the cross as the Son of God did. Both paths require the death of the flesh and a departure from paradise. Paradise is no longer an option, though people and religions still try to go there. In the second path, our spirits take dominance over our flesh in the painful way of the cross. Yet with the help of the great Holy Spirit, we are conformed to His image. It is not by way of paradise, as God had originally intended, but it is a table set before us in the presence of our enemies in the wilderness. The spirit takes preeminence in the path of the cross, as we walk the way of Jesus the only begotten Son of God. There the fallen self dies so we may be partakers of the divine nature through Jesus Christ. At the cross we begin our journey to heaven—starting with the kingdom of heaven within.

The other way, however, is the result of sin, the death of the flesh, by self-centeredness and self-destruction, and "self-godlikeness." It is the way of sin which leads to death. The death of the flesh by either way means that we must leave an earthly paradise behind. For those who choose to disobey God, this ultimate departure will lead to eternal separation from God in hell.

For those who choose the cross we go onto and into a new kingdom called heaven. We plant the kingdom of heaven on earth in our lives and prayers as the Son of God did, then enter heaven itself when we die. We must leave the untroubled abundance designed for the spirit, soul and body of Adam and Eve as provided in our first estate and first inheritance and become men and women of the spirit looking towards heavenly city whose Builder and Maker is God. The trip is difficult. But like the Author and Finisher of our faith, we, for the joy set before us endure the cross, to once again gain fellowship at the right hand of the throne of God with our Lord.

There were two trees in the center of the garden. Even in paradise there are choices. These trees are always at the center of life because choice is what God gave us, the essence of our being. The trees are not at the edge of the garden or our earthly walk. They are not hidden, nor obscure. One tree, the tree of the knowledge of good and evil daily draws us to its forbidden fruit. Satan is wrapped seductively in the middle of this tree. We can die in bondage at that tree in the present and eternally. At that tree ultimately choice is degraded and depleted through bondage to sin. The sinner dies in grave clothes of guilt, sin and iniquity; dead before the body dies. It is a tree of death with only evil rewards. The sinner will die eternally at this tree. Or, we can go to the other tree, so despised by the world, die there in the start of a new life, and pick up our crosses daily and live and die with Him. There we inherit eternal life in this world and the one which is to come. There is freedom from bondage at the cross: We die, sin dies, death dies, all made possible because He died. The One who was and is the Way, Truth and Life, knows us and shows us and draws us. At one tree we will die and live, the cross, and at the other we will live and die. From the cross where the Savior was nailed in humility and vulnerability, and through the resurrection, He calls us and waits in divine love. Come to Him now.

Excerpts of this chapter were taken from **Restoration NOW!,** by Nancy L. Eskijian, Copyright© 2011

CHAPTER FIFTEEN

The Veil is Rent

Behold a virgin shall be with child, and bear a Son, and they shall call His name Emmanuel, which being interpreted is, God with us. Matthew 1:23.

And behold, the veil of the temple was rent in twain from the top to the bottom; and the earth did quake, and the rocks rent. Matthew 27:51.

And it came to pass, that, while they communed together and reasoned, Jesus Himself drew near, and went with them. But their eyes were holden that they should not know Him. Luke 24:15-16.

And rend your heart, and not your garments, and turn unto the Lord your God; for He is gracious and merciful, slow to anger, and of great kindness, and repenteth Him of the evil. Joel 2:13.

I will surely rend the kingdom from thee, and will give it to thy servant. I Kings 11:11.

God is with us: How did it happen? Jesus took the form of flesh, so flesh could take the form of Him and be eternally bonded with the Creator. The rending of the veil is so many things. Let's take a look at the word "rend" for a minute. It means "to split or tear apart in pieces by violence." So when the veil separating the people from the holy of holies was "rent" it meant many things: The rending of old kingdoms and the establishment of a new one under the rulership of God; the escalation and acceleration of government and authority from an old order to a new world order. It meant that we would be kings and priests directly through the Mediator, Jesus Christ, our great High Priest. We are not separate from God Himself, because of the blood of Jesus. Suddenly God is reproduced in the hearts of men and women throughout the earth through the cross. God's kingdom could be established on this earth by a people transformed through the cross and the resurrection to be like their King, and then rule and reign with Him in His kingdom forever. It was a big, massive plan. The incorruptible Seed of God, Jesus Christ, could be planted in our hearts to create newness of life.

This exponential surge of divinity in the lives of believers came the day there was a rending of the veil of the temple, when the rocks were rent, when there was an earthquake on the earth and a heaven-quake in the spirit. An old order was destroyed and a new one set up. Saints came out of their graves and visited the old city, so believers could come out of their graves of sin and death and partake of the New Jerusalem. This changing of the guard could not be stopped. The effort to stop it through the crucifixion of Jesus, had only fixed and ensured its success, because the Seed had to die to reproduce. The kingdoms of this world were taken violently for all eternity (and the violent take it by force) from the prince of the power of the air and god of this world, as violence was done to Jesus. Also, the spiritual rulership of God's people, the Jews, had been ripped from their hands and given to a people who did not even know of or seek this position, the Gentiles. God gave new power and authority to the powerless: Weapons of warfare against principalities and ruling spirits, a new identity and authority in the name of Jesus, and the power of the blood applied to our hearts and lives. We were enabled by the blood of Jesus to serve the Living God instead of the kingdoms of sin, sickness, self and Satan. God had overruled the kingdoms of this world with the power of an endless life inserted into the spiritual genetics of a new race. Judgment had fallen on these kingdoms, later to be finally shaken and uprooted, but through the cross their power was defeated.

When the veil was rent the power, of the law, and the separation between Jew and Gentile, compelled by the law, were broken.

> That at that time ye were without Christ, being aliens from the commonwealth of Israel, and strangers from the covenants of promise, having no hope, and without God in the world: But now in Christ Jesus ye who sometimes were far off are made nigh by the blood of Christ. For He is our peace, who hath made both one, and hath broken down the middle wall of partition between us. Having abolished in His flesh the enmity, even the law of commandments, contained in ordinances; for to make in Himself of twain one new man, so making peace. And that He might reconcile both unto God in one body by the cross, having slain the enmity thereby: And came and preached peace to you which were afar off, and to them that were nigh, for through Him we both have access by one Spirit unto the Father. Ephesians 2:12-18.

The tearing apart or rending of Jesus' flesh was represented in the rending of the veil. Everyone could be reconciled to God. There were no more outsiders. We could all be recreated—there were no barriers between heaven and earth. Laws, practices, seasons, times, and kingdoms were transcended by a greater dimension of spiritual rule and authority. Racial, ethnic, social, economic, religious and gender barriers would be meaningless. A new unity was created under one body, one Spirit, one Lord, one baptism, one God and Father of all, who is above all, and through all, and in you all. God didn't do this by antichrist conformity stripping the world of its godly anointing, but by including the unique individuality of us all in His body and Spirit, cleansed by the blood. The world's systems, kingdoms and orders were suddenly destroyed one dark day on Calvary. The law of commandments was overshadowed by the law of love. We could be like our Creator, walking as He walked, loving as He loved, righteous as He is righteous, as He lived in and through us, born again and empowered by the Holy Spirit.

When the veil was rent, the power of the flesh was broken, the power of the devil was broken, the power of sin could ripped out of the human heart, as the heart of God was ripped open. The power of death was destroyed by death's own hand.

> Forasmuch as the children are partakers of flesh and blood, He also Himself likewise took part of the same; that through death He might destroy him that had the power of death, the devil; and deliver them who through fear of death were all their lifetime subject to bondage. Hebrews 2:14-15.

The power of the world, and its selfishness, divisions, and definitions ended by the power of love. The veils which keep us from the fullness of God and eternal life were torn down. The veil of sin, death, flesh, the world, the veil of religion and tradition were ripped out.

> He hath showed strength with His arm; He hath scattered the proud in the imagination of their hearts. He hath put down the mighty from their seats, and exalted them of low degree. He hath filled the hungry with good things; and the rich He hath sent empty away. Luke 1:51-53.

The first would be last and the last would be first. God was with us forever. God would not just be available to high priests in beautiful robes bearing symbols, signs and ephods, but a nation of kings and priests in His image and likeness would be given the same priestly and kingdom anointing to worship and serve Him. The new kings and priests would be clothed in His own righteousness, salvation, holiness, and minister Him through the power of the indwelling Holy Spirit.

He ripped through time. The veil of time and prophecy had witnessed fulfillment, for in Jesus Christ all the promises of God are yea and amen. He is the same yesterday, today and forever. He is Alpha and Omega, the Beginning and the Ending. In and through Him all time becomes the present, and the present reality of God erases time. The restraints of time were broken by the eternal One who now lives in us. God, beyond time, is with us, for us and in us. We have the power to become sons and daughters of God now, living in the presence of His eternal Spirit, through the power of an endless life.

The veil of Moses hid the glory of God from those who could not receive it. That veil is removed in Jesus Christ. The glory of God covering and filling our lives is restored through the grief and joy of the cross. Now we know what the knowledge of good and evil has cost—the death of God's Son Himself, so we could become sons of God.

> [12]Therefore, since we have such hope, we use great boldness of speech— [13]unlike Moses, who put a veil over his face so that the children of Israel could not look steadily at the end of what was passing away. [14]But their minds were blinded. For until this day the same veil remains unlifted in the reading of the Old Testament, because the veil is taken away in Christ. [15]But even to this day, when Moses is read, a veil lies on their heart. [16]Nevertheless when one turns to the Lord, the veil is taken away. 2 Corinthians 3:12 - 16 (NKJV).

The veil covered Moses' face so the children of Israel could not see the glory of God. The account in Exodus says that Moses' skin shone bright and that the children of Israel were afraid to come near him. Exodus 34:29-30. They were fearful of the glory of God. The law was more appealing to them than the glory, the flesh more than the spirit. However, the glory which shone on Moses' face told us of a time of fullness in Christ when we would behold His glory, and the glory would be in us, earthly vessels. The glory prophesied ending of the law, and the law's ways of dealing with sin, sickness, Satan and self that would be abolished one day. The Levitical priesthood with its earthly limitations came to an end. Jesus had established a new priesthood with new priests, new garments, with a new sacrifice, after the order of Melchizedek, not originating, or fathered or mothered by this earth.

Through grace and love we understand in part the depths of sorrow the Jesus experienced on the cross which reverses our sin, sickness and sorrow. He entered a tunnel of madness and sin at the cross through which God's love would draw us to His glory. When Satan confronted Jesus in the wilderness, he tempted Him to jump from the temple in presumption of God's protection, misapplying scripture of angelic protection of God's children of Psalms 91. Jesus jumped to His destruction at His own time in a free-fall of love at the cross as God's chosen sacrificial Lamb to redeem this world. By His own choice He disregarded His life and the protection He could have had, thereby glorifying the plan and purpose of the Father. Then Satan took Him on top of a high mountain and showed Him the kingdoms of this world, which he, Satan, would deliver to Jesus, along with their power and glory, if only Jesus would worship Him. But Jesus chose His own mountain, Calvary, and paid for those kingdoms with His own blood. Only God can truly deliver kingdoms, He is the only One, by His power and for His glory. Satan wanted to preempt this transfer of kingdoms by ungodly power, thereby making God subservient to him, and drawing the glory to the evil one. As I wrote earlier, Jesus would have become the Antichrist, for then Jesus would have ruled the world under Satan, salvation would have stopped, the plan of God ended, and the world set up for destruction. The Antichrist will be promised all the kingdoms of this world. Again Jesus agreed with God's divine ways and order.

Finally, Satan tempted Jesus to command the stones to be "made bread" when He was famished, but Jesus said man does not live by bread alone, but every word that proceeds out of the mouth of God. His meat always was to do the will of His Father—and that He did, at the beginning of His ministry and to the end of His own life, emptying Himself and not accepting the food of this world. He did not create bread in the temptation in the wilderness, to feed Himself. Instead He became the Bread of Life at the cross to feed the world. And here again we see the clash of kingdoms. Most people would rather "make bread" than be bread. The world, and those of the world, will manipulate the world for their purposes and "make bread." But those who follow Jesus, choose to release their lives to be bread, and in so doing, be crushed and broken into a refined state to feed others. This is the divide of humanity; a self centered life or a God centered life.

It was the original intent of God in creation that we experience and live in the glory of God. But when man sinned, "Ichabod," "the glory has departed" was written over an unworthy temple. Still, God had a plan. The Ark of the Covenant had returned through the new covenant of the cross, by a true King, like David. So the rending of the veil returned the glory to lost creation. Life can be blessed, not cursed. Sickness can be reversed and sin eradicated. Self comes down from being a god, and dies at the cross with the true Son of God, so in His shame we may gain His glory. Satan is put under our feet as we abide in Him.

Jesus, our great High Priest, enters the holy of holies for us and rips the veil separating the people from their God. "This hope we have as an anchor of the soul, both sure and steadfast, and which enters the Presence behind the veil, where the forerunner has entered for us, even Jesus, having become High Priest forever according to the order of Melchizedek." Hebrews 6:19-20. The mystery is revealed in heaven and in us, for the holy transaction of the blood, that all may enter in. It is the new covenant with all of us. God had been separated from His creation for too long. He desired to love them closely and intimately. The veil blocked that intimacy, for He wants to know us and be known.

When Jesus entered His ministry He emptied the temple of its ungodly merchandise and clutter. Now He tears down the temple made with human hands as the temple of His body is raised in three days. He opens the way for a temple of lively stones to be made with hearts of flesh through His endless priesthood. Jesus is both radical and revolutionary. Everything is reconciled in Christ and we in Him and He in us. We enter in the veil with our High Priest. The glory would be no longer be frightening to God's people, but is now accessible to containers recreated in the image of God who can receive it. This veil was torn from the top down. The tearing of the veil, as original creation, was an act of God alone. God demonstrated from the beginning to end that salvation could only come by His own hand, whether it was by the animal slain to cover Adam and Eve or by the Lamb slain at Calvary.

The veil of His flesh was rent, as the heart of God was opened so we might enter in.

> Therefore, brethren, having boldness to enter the Holiest by the blood of Jesus, by a new and living way which He consecrated for us, through the veil, that is, His flesh, and having a High Priest over the house of God, let us draw near with a true heart in full assurance of faith, having our hearts sprinkled from an evil conscience and our bodies washed with pure water. Hebrews 10:19-22.

And so, a new and living way is made possible through the torn veil of Jesus' flesh on the cross. His flesh was cut and torn like other sacrifices foretelling of His death, sacrifices at the hands of other, less famous priests than Annas and Caiaphas, so true priests could be raised up. Had God not been broken, then we could not have been put back together again and come to His fullness, walking and living through Him.

At the same time flesh which blinds our eyes to the things of God is eternally rent at the cross for us, too. Our hearts are rent so He may enter in. This is the rending of the hearts and not the garments, because God does not look at the outward appearance but at the heart. Our outward show cannot bring salvation or repentance. He is not interested in a religious tearing of clothes, but a humble and contrite heart. We've got to break open our hearts before God.

Finally, there is another veil waiting to be lifted because of the cross. An eternal relationship waits to be consummated. That is the marriage between Jesus and His bride because of the cross. Jesus has been waiting for His bride for a long time. He is longing like Jacob for His Rachel. The church has been His Leah, but the Bride His Rachel. Jacob waited seven years. Leah was fruitful and did her part in building the kingdom, but His heart longs for the lovely Rachel and the new marriage celebration. Perhaps that is an end time message, when Jesus comes again, first for, and then with His bride after the Great Tribulation. At the cross the new marriage covenant was cut, and He paid with His blood—that's His dowry. In this dispensation the Holy Spirit moves as a wind across the earth to woo the bride and bring her to His feet as Ruth to her Boaz. At the foot of the cross we are given the opportunity become at one again with our Maker, betrothed as Husband and wife, forsaking all others, vowing to love, honor, cherish and obey, so that the glory He had with the Father from the foundation of the world may be ours. John 17:21-22. Someday the bridal veil will be lifted and Christ and His bride may be in total union and fellowship at the marriage supper of the Lamb, but for the time being the bride does not know her Bridegroom in totality. Through the veil of time she is being grafted into Him and transformed into His image, until such day of which John writes, "(B)ut we know that, when He shall appear, we shall be like Him; for we shall see Him as He is." I John 3:2. Likewise Paul states, "(N)ow I know in part; but then shall I know even as also I am known." I Corinthians 13:11. Now we see through a glass darkly, but then we behold His face in righteousness, and awake with His likeness. Psalms 17:15. Today the cross is the down payment on the lifting of this veil.

Many veils vanished at the cross. Once our eyes were "holden" and we did not know Him. The men on the road to Emmaus could not see Him until He imparted the knowledge of Himself to them. But in these last days of revelation, He is revealed and allows Himself to be revealed by the mighty Holy Spirit. The closer His return, the more the eyes of our understanding will be enlightened that we may know the hope of our calling in Him and the riches of the glory of His inheritance in the saints. This is because He wants His body to do the greater works. He wants to form us to be "sons of God," so the sons of God may be manifest to the world, until the Son of God appears, and then they shall see Him as He is. Today He wants us to go into the highways and byways and compel them to come into the marriage feast, so that the marriage will be furnished with guests. His heart holds the whole world. He opens the mystery and opens Himself in desperate love to show us who He is. To this end He rends the veil to His presence, so He may love us and transform us to love in His name, for that is the reason why He came.

> The door of love is opened wide
> Jesus calls the world inside
> The veil is lifted from our eyes
> He calls us, His eternal bride.

CHAPTER SIXTEEN

Manifesto of the Blood

For the life of the flesh is in the blood: and I have given it to you upon the altar to make an atonement for your souls: for it is the blood that maketh an atonement for the soul. Leviticus 17:11.

And to Jesus the mediator of the new covenant, and to the blood of sprinkling, that speaketh better things than that of Abel. Hebrews 12:24.

For this is my blood of the new testament, which is shed for many for the remission of sins. Matthew 26:28.

Unto Him that loved us, and washed us from our sins in His own blood. Revelation 3:5.

When we consider the blood of Jesus, we are meditating upon a most holy subject, for the blood of Jesus is that substance which carries the very life of God the Son, God in the flesh, to the world. As the scriptures say, the life is in the blood. The blood of Jesus is supernatural blood which, when applied to the sins and breaches of the world, will enable the redemption and re-creation of new men and women for a new heaven and new earth. By necessity it had to be shed, or the world would simply self-destruct. Sin was by choice, and redemption must also be by choice. So, the blood is shed that we may wash our robes of filth and sin and make them white by the blood of the Lamb. Can there be any greater than a Creator and Savior who loved us and washed us from our sins in His own blood? When the Lamb who was slain, is found worthy to break the seven seals releasing judgments on the earth, opening the way for Christ's final reclamation and redemption of the planet, all heaven and earth breaks into worship. Revelation 5:

> ⁸And when he had taken the book, the four beasts and four *and* twenty elders fell down before the Lamb, having every one of them harps, and golden vials full of odors, which are the prayers of saints. ⁹And they sung a new song, saying, Thou art worthy to take the book, and to open the seals thereof: for thou wast slain, and hast redeemed us to God by thy blood out of every kindred, and tongue, and people, and nation;... ¹³And every creature which is in heaven, and on the earth, and under the earth, and such as are in the sea, and all that are in them, heard I saying, Blessing, and honor, and glory, and power, *be* unto him that sitteth upon the throne, and unto the Lamb for ever and ever.

There is a reason for His worthiness and a reason for His worship. He is worthy because, as the Lamb slain from the foundation of the world He took all the judgments, sins and the curses of this world, collectively and individually, at the cross. His blood was shed for salvation. Nevertheless His sacrifice has been despised and rejected for the most part. This time the world's blood will be shed in judgment because it rejected His blood for salvation at the cross. Because the blood of God the Son, King of Kings and Lord of Lords, touched and cleanses the earth, He alone may release judgments from heaven to earth. He alone can open the seals. Yes, there is worship for His worthiness. But there is also worship for God's ultimate plan. The judgments are for many purposes and the judgments will lead to the final redemption of the earth when all things are put under His feet. The massive worship of all creatures in heaven and earth signified that the curse would be over.

We see the triumph of the blood in Revelation, but let's start in

Genesis. The first shedding of blood takes place after the disaster of the original sin in the Garden. To cover their newly discovered shame, Adam and Eve sewed together fig leaves as aprons. It was a temporary, superficial, and immature solution. Despite their spiritual blindness even these two knew that the weakness, limitations, and shame of the flesh now had to be covered. Subsequently, God Himself set in motion a pattern which would be completed by the sacrifice of His own Son as the ultimate Covering, when He killed animals to clothe the bodies of Adam and Eve. The word says, "Unto Adam also and to his wife did the Lord God make coats of skins, and clothed them." Therefore, we can conclude from the word "skins" a number of animals died and their blood was shed, to provide clothing for Adam and Eve. (Curious "skins" is "sin" plus "kins" in English—our Kinsman Redeemer?) There was the first shedding of innocent blood as man sinned against God. It is significant that animals would die, and the job could not be accomplished with just one. The pattern of killing innocent animals to cover human guilt had just begun. These animals covered the guilt and the shame of the sinners by the shedding of their blood, but their death did not erase the sin. And so the world waited for the Son.

The temporary aprons that Adam and Eve crafted would never have provided a covering, because the leaves gave no protection, warmth, or security for the two that were soon to leave Eden. God furnished them garments, robes to wear, as they had lost the covering of the glory of God and were to be driven into the environment of the world where they would live by their own sweat and blood. They choose to be as gods, plurality, divided, and so now must face the consequences of living by the knowledge of good and evil which had been acquired at the forbidden tree. God shows us that if you want to be a *god* instead of a *child* of God, you are on your own. Even then, God made a covering for them and did not leave them without some form of mercy. True, these were coverings denoting the lower nature, animal skins, rather than the higher nature, the glory of God, but the temporary protection was an earthly gift.

The fixation of permanent things and patterns emerge as man and woman leave Eden to create a bulwark and a protection against the hostility of the environment. Something new had to be contended with, death, and fortresses would be built against it, until Jesus came. Death, time, decay, danger, isolation, all of these were some of the new enemies—not to mention the internal enemy called sin that would take their second son, Abel. Death came with the loss of eternal life, and the incorporation of the limitations of the tree of the knowledge of good and evil. In the meanwhile, God would preserve them, and, in the course of time, institute the law whereby life could be preserved, orders fixed, and stability provided. Proverbs 16:6 states: "By mercy and truth iniquity is purged: and by the fear of the Lord men depart from evil." God by His mercy and truth began the process which would end in iniquity being purged by the power of the blood of His Son: The mercy—Adam and Eve did not deserve the provision; the truth—only God could provide the covering; and so it is with the sacrifice of Jesus.

Had they feared God, the sacrifice would not have been required. As Samuel told Saul when Saul sacrificed the animals that were supposed to be slaughtered from the Amalekites:

> Hath the Lord as great delight in burnt offerings and sacrifices, as in obeying the voice of the Lord? Behold, to obey is better than sacrifice, and to hearken than the fat of rams. I Samuel 15:22.

Why? Simply because something will die because of disobedience. If nothing else, a part of you will die in disobeying God. Furthermore, the disobedience opens the door for demonic attack and curses to be placed on the sinner and generations thereafter. One thing that will be sacrificed is your life. It is an unfaithfulness leading to death. For restoration to God Samuel was telling Saul that the Lord's delight is not in the burnt offerings and sacrifices—these are representations of human disregard and betrayal of God and are wounds on the innocent. But even more, the Lord knew that each animal killed, and the bewildering pain they experienced, was a type of His Son that would be slain, and the blood that was required for a final cleansing and redemption of the world. What the scripture means is that in each act of disobedience a part of God had to die on the cross, because a part of our spirit in the image of God dies in disobedience to the Lord.

The second breach in the spirit and breach in creation came with the murder of Abel by Cain. This was a trespass against man, while the original sin was a sin against God. As the scriptural account goes, Abel offered to God a more acceptable sacrifice than Cain; it was a sacrifice of the firstlings of the flock and the "fat of these." God had respect to Abel's sacrifice. Both the sacrifice presented by Abel to God and the sacrifice of Abel himself match the appointed pattern. Later Abel's murder by a jealous brother who wanted to maintain his own system of righteousness, prophesied of the sacrifice of the Lamb to come. The murder of Jesus would be by jealous "brothers" who wanted to maintain their own religious system in opposition to righteousness established by God alone. Cain brought the works of his hand, which God did not accept, and Cain was angry. Had God accepted Cain's sacrifices, He would have made the blood of Jesus of none effect. He was willing to allow the death of Abel to maintain the purity of the pattern of the blood. It had to be preserved in type until the fulfillment of Jesus. The scripture says Cain's countenance fell. It is clear that the way had been pointed out to Cain, and God reminded him that if you do well, you will be accepted, but if not, sin lies at the door. There is no compromise with the blood. The blood and the pattern of the blood separates us from the world, the world's system, the world's religions, and the world's judgment.

In rage Cain killed Abel. One translation of the New Testament states,

> Because this is the message which you have heard from the beginning, namely, We should habitually be loving one another with a divine and self-sacrificial love; not even as Cain who was out of the Pernicious One, and killed his brother by severing his jugular vein. And on what account did he kill him? Because his works were pernicious and those of his brother righteous. I John 3:11-12 *Wuest, New Testament.*

It is interesting that severing the jugular vein would be prophetic of the animals slaughtered by the millions under the law. It is also interesting to note that from the very beginning the message was to love one another, for love is the repairer of the breach, and the restorer of paths to dwell in. In fact, it is the path in which we must live as we abide in Him. Jude writes (v.21), "Keep yourselves in the love of God." Jesus says, "Thou shalt love the Lord thy God with all thy heart, and with all thy soul and with all thy mind, and thou shalt love thy neighbor as thyself." Matthew 22:37-38.

After Cain killed Abel and buried him in the ground,

> [9]...the LORD said to Cain, "Where *is* Abel your brother?" He said, "I do not know. *Am* I my brother's keeper?" [10]And He said, "What have you done? The voice of your brother's blood cries out to Me from the ground. [11]So now you *are* cursed from the earth, which has opened its mouth to receive your brother's blood from your hand. [12]When you till the ground, it shall no longer yield its strength to you. A fugitive and a vagabond you shall be on the earth." Genesis 4:9-12.

Innocent blood will always cry from the ground. The blood cries from the soil of our hearts when we have been wounded. The blood of civil wars, genocide, and domestic violence cries out. The blood of wounded children whose emotions have been torn apart cries out. The blood of the unborn who are aborted cries out. Whenever there is a wound, it will cry out. The wound may not literally yield blood. There may not be literal buried bodies. But blood has life and it cries when it shed by sin. That which violates life and creation will cry out. Trespasses against our brothers and sisters in anger, slander, curses, and corrupt communication, hits, wounds, murders, and bruises will cry out.

The blood of Abel is the blood of a wounded planet which is buried in the earth. Man's way of dealing with trespasses against a brother is to bury it. We hide from God, or make flimsy excuses as we sin against Him, but we bury our grudges against one another. The thing is, sin cannot be hidden because the cries of the blood will always be heard. So, only something greater can cancel the power of this blood in the earth. The cries will not stop by ignoring them—they will only be stopped one day in judgment or mercy.

That is judgment for sin or mercy at the cross. Accordingly, we are told in the book of Hebrews of the "blood of sprinkling," the blood of Jesus, "that speaks better things than that of Abel." The blood of Jesus can erase our sins and wipe out our iniquities. That blood can heal the wounds that cry out because that blood has supernatural power to repair creation and make it as though the breach did not happen by transcending the breach. The blood of Jesus can reach through time and heal and make whole. The blood of Jesus makes us new again and cleanses our souls.

The blood sacrifices would continue during the time of patriarchs, Noah, Abraham, Isaac, and Jacob. A prophetically complete picture of the cross is seen in Abraham's offering of Isaac on Mt. Moriah, The father, Abraham, obedient to God and trusting even in the resurrection of his son, offered his promised son, Isaac, as a sacrifice. The child carried his own wood for the sacrifice and surrendered his body to the knife of his father, when the Heavenly Father intervened with the ram in the thicket, prophetic of the Lamb provided for all eternity. Although Abraham offered his son in a monumental act of faith, God did not take him up on the offer completely. You see, the highest sacrifice would be the Father's sacrifice of His Son Jesus. Even though Abraham's obedience was a type, Abraham could not share this ultimate glory.

In Egypt, a new pattern was developed and a feast established in anticipation of the law, called the Passover. The Passover was another complete picture of the sacrifice and the blood to come. Each household was to take a lamb according to the number of persons in the house on the tenth day of the first month of the year. The lamb would be a male of the first year without blemish. The lamb would be kept until the fourteenth day of that month and the whole assembly of Israel would kill their lambs at the same time in the evening. The blood of that lamb was to be struck on the two doorposts and the upper lintel of the houses of the home where the lamb was eaten. It would be roasted in fire, not raw or boiled in water, its head with its legs and the all the extension of it was roasted. Nothing was to remain until morning. Then, when the angel of death passed <u>through</u> the land of Egypt, the angel would see the blood on the lintel and the two side posts of the door. The Lord would pass <u>over</u> that house:

> [12]For I will pass through the land of Egypt on that
> night, and will strike all the firstborn in the land of
> Egypt, both man and beast; and against all the
> gods of Egypt I will execute judgment: I *am* the LORD.
> [13]Now the blood shall be a sign for you on the
> houses where you *are*. And when I see the blood,
> I will pass over you; and the plague shall not be on
> you to destroy *you* when I strike the land of Egypt.
> Exodus 12:12 - 13 (NKJV).

We know that in the larger sense, God's household, His creation, would be saved by the death of Jesus, and, likewise, in microcosm, each believer has the promise that they and their household would be saved. The lamb was to be taken for each household. Significantly, it would be taken into the house in the new first month, speaking of creation, new beginnings, and redemption. That lamb would be set apart on the tenth of the month and taken into the household, and sacrificed on the fourteenth. This animal was to be a familiar, chosen and loved lamb, and it would be killed by the family's own hand. It was a lamb that was personally valuable and could have had promise in advancing the natural life of the flock. But it is given to God to advance the spiritual life of His flock and preserve the knowledge of God of its owners. The whole assembly of Israel killed their lambs at once, just as Israel and the world would kill their Lamb, Jesus Christ, at one time. There was no haphazard strategy. The death of the lambs came in the evening, and even though Jesus was killed during the day, darkness covered this event. The lamb was to be a first year male without spot or blemish like our Lord, the first fruits of God and from the dead. The blood was drained from the lamb, it was not burnt with the body. The body experiences destruction and the body is eaten to provide strength for the journey out of Egypt, but the blood is poured out to be placed over each door in the sign of a cross, so that when the angel of death passed through, it would pass over the homes of the children of Israel.

The flesh of Jesus died on the cross, and all flesh must be dethroned and dies at the cross. The flesh of Jesus carries our sorrows, sickness, and self, and there at the cross we leave our sorrow, sickness, and self. When we take of the communion bread, representing the broken then resurrected body of our Lord, the life of God is ministered to our bodies and souls. Not only is new life provided for our own bodies, but a new body in which we may live is given to us, the body of Christ. Ultimately, one day we will have a new resurrection body. When we take the communion cup, the blood of Jesus is applied to our spirits to make us one with the Father again through the purging of sin and the cleansing power of the blood. The blood of Jesus is our protection when the angel of judgment on sin and eternal death pass over; the blood of Jesus is our protection. We obtain the supernatural power of the Son of God through the blood because the flesh has no power.

One last point, the body of the lamb was to be roasted in the fire, not raw or boiled in water. The body of the Lamb of God goes through the fire of affliction and judgment. It is not untested as raw flesh, and not simply boiled in water which has no flavor. The whole offering is given, no part is left out, and it is given at the furnace of the cross.

The blood sacrifices are described in detail under the law. Of the five great sacrificial offerings, the burnt offering, the sin offering, the meal offering, the trespass offering, the peace offering, four will require the shedding of blood, because without the shedding of blood there is no remission, or freedom from sin, or deliverance from the penalty, of sin. Many studies have described the depths of these offerings and found a picture of the sacrifice of the Lord Jesus. In the burnt offering, He first of all offers Himself wholly to God in consecration. In the sin offering we have a picture of Him becoming sin who knew no sin. In the trespass offering He takes away our trespasses that occur as we walk in the flesh. The meal offering is an act of acknowledging God's goodness. And finally, in the peace offering there is peace between God and man and man and man through the blood of the cross. "For by one offering He hath perfected forever them that are sanctified." Hebrews 10:14. All at once old covenants and old testaments are transcended. In three days the temple is destroyed and the temple of His body raised, and in three days the work of the blood is perfected, so we may perfected. In three days the temple on earth becomes our bodies as He places the blood on the mercy seat, and we have access through His blood to enter into the holy of holies.

> But Christ being come an high priest of good things to come, by a greater and more perfect tabernacle, not made with hands, that is to say, not of this building; neither by the blood of goats and calves, but by His own blood He entered in once into the holy place, having obtained eternal redemption for us. For is the blood of bulls and of goats and the ashes of an heifer sprinkling the unclean sanctifieth to the purifying of the flesh; How much more shall the blood of Christ, who through the eternal Spirit offered Himself without spot to God, purge your conscience from dead works to serve the living God? And for this cause He is the mediator of the new testament that by means of death, for the redemption of the transgressions that were under the first testament, that which are called might receive the promise of eternal inheritance. Hebrews 9:11-15.

And as the old testament was dedicated with blood, Moses sprinkling the book of the law and the people, saying, "This is the blood of the testament which God hath enjoined unto you," and he also sprinkled the tabernacle, and the vessels of ministry, we are told, "almost all things are by the law purged with blood; and without shedding of blood is no remission." Hebrews 9:22.

God had enjoined the law to the people by the sprinkling of blood, and sanctifying the temple on earth. Now we are told that the patterns of these things are purified in the heavens with a better sacrifice than that of calves and goats—Jesus Christ. Christ is joined to us eternally by the blood.

Note that the people of God were instructed not to "eat" the blood in the sacrifices of animals, but to drain the blood out. Why, because you take on the "life" of the flesh in the blood, and our "life" is not in burnt sacrifices of animals. But Jesus tells us explicitly that we should "drink" His blood as well as eat His flesh.

[53]Then Jesus said to them, "Most assuredly, I say to

you, unless you eat the flesh of the Son of Man and drink His blood, you have no life in you. [54]Whoever eats My flesh and drinks My blood has eternal life, and I will raise him up at the last day. [55]For My flesh is food indeed, and My blood is drink indeed. [56]He who eats My flesh and drinks My blood abides in Me, and I in him. [57]As the living Father sent Me, and I live because of the Father, so he who feeds on Me will live because of Me. [58]This is the bread which came down from heaven—not as your fathers ate the manna, and are dead. He who eats this bread will live forever." John 6: 53-58 (NKJV).

Why, because we are to take on the life of God Himself, because we are created in the image of God. We take on the life of the Son of God, so we can be sons of God, not animals, but sons of God.

Yes, these great words are written in the book of Hebrews:

[23]Therefore *it was* necessary that the copies of the things in the heavens should be purified with these, but the heavenly things themselves with better sacrifices than these. [24]For Christ has not entered the holy places made with hands, *which are* copies of the true, but into heaven itself, now to appear in the presence of God for us; [25]not that He should offer Himself often, as the high priest enters the Most Holy Place every year with blood of another— [26]He then would have had to suffer often since the foundation of the world; but now, once at the end of the ages, He has appeared to put away sin by the sacrifice of Himself. Hebrews 9:23 - 26 (NKJV).

Final and complete, sacred and holy, the blood sacrifice, is made once and for all by our Lord Jesus Christ on our behalf. A new covenant is cut at the cross by the death and resurrection of the very One who cuts the covenant. We partake of this sacrifice, and eat this sacrifice and are washed in the blood of this sacrifice, and the impartations of all the sacrifices cut and split open and the shedding of their blood at once become ours.

He is the consummation of all the blood of the prophets from Abel to Zechariah, and more. He did not point to a greater day, but was that Daystar on high. We are purchased by His blood, saved through faith in His blood, justified by His blood, and redeemed by His blood. He sprinkles the nations with His blood, the holy places in heaven, and our hearts which He makes holy and writes His own word of salvation.

> Now may the God of peace, that brought again from the dead our Lord Jesus that great shepherd of the sheep, through the blood of the everlasting covenant, make you perfect in every good work to do His will, working in you that which is well-pleasing in His sight, through Jesus Christ; to whom be glory, forever and ever. Amen. Hebrews 13:20-21.

Those who accept the blood will be joined to the Father in an everlasting covenant. Yet, because many will reject this blood, rivers again will flow with blood in the judgment of this earth.

This is the power of the blood. There is no other name under heaven by which we must be saved. By the blood our inheritance is redeemed. A transfusion of eternal life is released at the cross through the blood and by the living bread, His body, which He gives for the life of the world. The blood restores holiness, order, preservation, and eternal life to creation by closing the breaches and repairing the destruction of sin. The blood is our red carpet to the throne room of God. Jesus is our holy Way and only Way. It is a free gift. Do not despise the new inheritance provided by Jesus. You are not redeemed with corruptible things, but by the precious blood of the Lamb. Your redemption and life will not come with fame or money or power or relationships, but by the supernatural power of the blood. By the blood we enter the holy of holies, a new and living way made possible by Jesus. Someday He will return with His vesture dipped in blood, a fitting garment from the very gates of Eden to Revelation to redeem once and for all a lost planet.

CHAPTER SEVENTEEN

The Intercession of the Cross
The Blood Prayer He Prayed
by His Death

[10]Yet it pleased the LORD to bruise *him*; he hath put him to grief: when thou shalt make his soul an offering for sin, he shall see his seed, he shall prolong his days, and the pleasure of the LORD shall prosper in his hand. [11]He shall see of the travail of his soul, and shall be satisfied: by his knowledge shall my righteous servant justify many; for he shall bear their iniquities. [12]Therefore will I divide him *a portion* with the great, and he shall divide the spoil with the strong; because he hath poured out his soul unto death: and he was numbered with the transgressors; and he bare the sin of many, and made intercession for the transgressors. Isaiah 53:10 - 12.

Thy kingdom come. Thy will be done in earth, as it is in heaven. Matthew 6:10.

On earth as it is in heaven: Jesus intercedes in heaven and we intercede on earth. In between, Jesus interceded, hanging between heaven and earth at the cross. This is the blood prayer of the cross. What is prayer? Prayer is praying out the totality of what

Jesus purchased by His blood on the cross. His prayers in heaven are the essential activity of the Son and our prayers on earth are an essential activity of His body. When He stops praying, the judgment that could have been averted by the cross will come.

Before we get to the blood prayer, we need to understand the basics of intercession: Intercession means "to strike upon," or "against". We do a lot of damage against the plans of the enemy when we pray and also the kingdom of heaven suffers violence—there is much opposition to the kingdom of heaven, but the violent take it by force, we storm heaven.

Intercession also means "to assail with petitions," "to urge," and when on behalf of another, "to intercede." The Latin root intercede means "to come between," which has the somewhat opposed meanings of "obstruct" and "to interpose on behalf of" a person, and finally "to intercede—bringing the parties together."

Intercession means to come between, to bring people to God and His will, and come between, in order to separate and obstruct people from the will of the enemy and their own delusions. We pray to bring the will of God into a situation and pray that Satan's will cannot rule over the flesh nor the world. We pray in order to join to God's will and separate from Satan's will.

Because God's will and word are settled in heaven, there is no doubt about what He wants. But there are clearly obstacles to the materialization of His will. For example, as believers we battle spiritual forces in the second heaven where Satan rules. Sometimes prayer serves to overcome the flesh, attitudes and mindset in opposition to the word of God, emotional history and soul ties, and sometimes we are just doing business in the world. Prayer releases the supernatural power of God into the natural and demonic realm.

Intercession is priestly prayer. It is prayer by those who know God and know what the heart of God desires. Intercessors are the agents of God's will on earth as it is in heaven. Jesus is the agent of God's will in heaven as He is our Advocate and ever lives to make intercession, so there is constant communication between heaven and earth in prayer because of the blood. We are doing the work of the Father and the will of the Father on earth and calling down the will and work of the Father through prayer in agreement with the Son.

Therefore, the first great pillar of intercession and center of all prayer is, "Thy Kingdom come thy will be done on earth as it is in heaven." It is no mistake that phrase is in the middle of the Lord's Prayer. Prayer is the vehicle for the will of God to be released in the earth realm. That means the intercessor understands the will of God and stands in the place of God on earth. Jesus isn't on earth any more, we are, we are His body, we have the same Holy Spirit and we are seated with Him in heavenly places.

The second great pillar is that intercession is the function of the priest. The Bible says we are kings and priests. A priest stands in the gap between God and man. The priestly prayer belongs to priests, and the function of the priest was to be an intermediary and a connection between man and God, to release God's will, to avert God's judgment in mercy, to worship, to sacrifice and more. God wants to turn us into priests so we can be priests for others. Jesus is our Great High Priest.

All believers have the ministry of intercession, though all believers don't take up the ministry of intercession. We have the Holy Spirit and the Holy Spirit gives us vision and insight and truth, the Holy Spirit leads us into all truth. The meaning of priest is not a religious one, it means we are set aside and holy and because of Christ in us and the Holy Spirit in us. Being a child of the Father, we have a different role in this world than other people who do not have the Spirit of God working in them. We all have a calling and that calling is to pray. That is the calling of the blood bought church. The blood implores us to pray.

Priests plead for man. Priests go to God and say, look this man, this woman is not perfect—they need help, or protect them until they can come to their senses. This person has sinned or has lifestyle of sin which is destructive, please Lord intervene. This city needs salvation and this nation needs to come back to God. This church needs help in these areas. This person is in pain or sick or out of order, and Lord, release your mercy, release your healing, release your wisdom, release your kingdom. This person needs protection on the job, or while driving, or protect their home. This person may be in danger, or need of help, the priest will go to heaven for that person. The priest stands in the gap for divine order, divine will and favor, divine protection, divine healing.

As intercessors, we have to go to heaven for that person because they don't know how to do it for themselves, or we must stand in the gap for them, or God tells us to help them. Perhaps they are weak or ungodly or a child or don't know any better. A lot of people have no knowledge of God and they are vulnerable to the enemy and the law of sin and death is in motion, and can't help themselves. Sometimes they are caught off guard, but God raises up others to pray, and so we pray. And every believer taking the kingdom by force needs the power of intercessory prayer.

A priest helps people return to God. The priest also comes between a person and the power of the death and the enemy. The priest stops the law of sin and death, which is constantly working attracting demons, generating curses, and interrupts it with the law of the spirit of life in Christ Jesus. Therefore a priest brings things together and also separates, just as Jesus, our Great High Priest does. He brings us back to God and He separates us from the world, the flesh and the devil. He wants us joined to the will of God and separated from the will of the enemy, the flesh or the world. This takes the power of the cross and the resurrection. Without Jesus as the great Intercessor, nothing would happen. His work on the cross paved the way for all intercession.

The Bible tells us that we are kings and priests. Outwardly, spiritual headship in the earth realm is administered through kings, but divine government and compassion, working on the inner man, comes through priests so that we can become kings. The king deals with the outward man, and has gained authority in this world because of the priest. The priest deals with the inner man and the spirit. The priest brings healing, the priest brings holiness, the priest gives divine order and truth inwardly, and when these take root, then we can operate as kings, the head and not the tail, instead of trying to figure out life every minute and not knowing who we are. The priest connects the heart of man with the heart of God. In God's kingdom, there is the holiness first, before ruling. A lot of people want God's blessings and favor and all that He offers. But He extends His favor first by changing us, so we can receive favor. The world is in desperate need of the holy.

A priest helps in this way as shown in Hebrews 5:1:

> ¹For every high priest taken from among men is ordained for men in things *pertaining* to God.

What does that mean? The priest is separated from other men and women in things that belong to God. God becomes the focus—we live a life with our eyes on heaven and our Heavenly Father. The church is not like everyone out there. If you are a believer, under the new covenant you are a priest and you are set apart for God… and the things that pertain, that he may offer both gifts and sacrifices for sins:

> ²Who can have compassion on the ignorant, and on them that are out of the way; for that he himself also is compassed with infirmity. Hebrews 5:2.

Jesus experienced our human experience so He could be our priest. He had compassion on our weakness, and He was there to help those who were ignorant or out of the way, in other words, lost their path. This is not all the time, but sometimes when we pray for people, people are ignorant of the promises of God or the power of God. They are ignorant of the fact, for example, that they need protection, or that they can be healed, or that they need to steer clear of some people. They are ignorant of the consequences of sin and disobedience. They are ignorant that they can open themselves to curses, open themselves to demons and pass all this on for generations. They are ignorant of the promises of God and other things, and don't know the ways of God, or they are out of the way, they got lost and they need the Holy Spirit and the laborers of God to get them back on the path. All kinds of people are ignorant and out of the way. That's not every time we pray, but sometimes and so the priest stands in the gap. The priest is a shepherd to bring the sheep back to the way.

Ignorant people don't know that what they are doing or not doing can hurt them personally as well as other people—there are a whole lot of ignorant people in the world and in the church. They are ignorant of the harm they can create, they are ignorant of the word, they are ignorant of the consequences of their thoughts, words and actions, they are ignorant of the curses that follow, they are ignorant of the enemy, they are ignorant of demons and spiritual warfare. They are just plain ignorant. People in the church are ignorant and out of the way. Just coming to church does not impart wisdom alone; you need to study the word on your own and get into prayer. The Bible tells us to get wisdom, get understanding.

People out of the way, are out of the Way, the Truth and the Life. Being out of the way of the Way, the Truth and the Life is being ignorant and out of the way or rejecting the Way, Truth and Life. So the priest that knows the will of God, prays and sacrifices his life at times to bring them back. That is what priests do.

But all intercession has one great heart and center. Intercession is the work of the cross—this is very important.

> Therefore I will divide Him a portion with the great, And He shall divide the spoil with the strong, Because He poured out His soul unto death, And He was numbered with the transgressors, And He bore the sin of many, And made intercession for the transgressors. Isaiah 53:12 (NKJV).

What is the word saying? By Jesus dying on the cross, He bore our sins and His very death made intercession for the transgressors, in other words, His death was the door to all the salvation and heaven that we as sinners needed to come to the throne of grace of the Father. Jesus did the ultimate work of intercession on the cross, He joined us to God by the blood, and He separated us from death, hell and the grave, the power and penalty of sin, the flesh, the world and the devil by the blood. His death itself, by bearing our sins, was intercession—standing in the gap for the entire human race.

Jesus stood in the gap by prayers and by His very death for the whole human race. He prayed by His death. He interceded, made a way by His death. His death was an offering to God as a sacrifice and prayer to accept that sacrifice. He stood in the gap for the human race by His death. He put His blood on the mercy seat in heaven, the very temple in heaven. Jesus put His blood there, so we could always come to the Father to the throne of grace. Since the blood was there, the Father had to recognize anyone who came by way of the blood. The divine death was the only way to the Father.

Like Jesus, sometimes our daily sacrifice is a living prayer. Our love is a living prayer, because we are offering up to God on behalf of others. We are saying, don't you see, God loves you and by this anointing of love, He is calling you closer to Him. Our hearts are pleading in love for another person or a city or a family. Our love and obedience is intercession, because we are showing people in our lives, this is the way, walk ye in it. Our heart is crying out to heaven for them by our love and our sacrifice. Sacrifice is the highest prayer. Intercession is about a sacrifice; it is about getting the full value of the sacrifice that Jesus provided.

Sacred power is being transferred to those who are unclean, disobedient, confused or ignorant. There is a transfer from the holy to the unholy. Jesus takes our guilt, so we can take His holiness. He takes our sickness, so we can take His health. He takes our death, so we can take His life. He takes our sinful condition, so we can take His holy eternal one, so there is a transference in deed which occurs later in prayer.

The story of a pearl: A pearl is produced by an oyster, and it takes a little grain of sand in that oyster to produce the pearl. The oyster doesn't ask for it, but the oyster is created for it. A little sand enters the oyster when it is open and creates an irritation. Over a period of time the oyster secretes a mineral substance to cover that irritation of the sand, then the pearl is formed. That is the oyster's life. The oyster doesn't ask for the sand, but the sand is in the environment in which it lives—it is in the water it processes at the floor of the ocean. What should be a constant problem to the oyster, becomes a process of beauty.

We live in an environment of constant sand, irritation, people who are angry, people who don't know the will of God, relatives who are lost, politics that need reformation, a nation that has departed from God. That irritates our souls, we are vexed, but when we pray, something beautiful is formed in us, that pearl of great price, the kingdom, and then something beautiful happens for the people we lift up in prayer. It is because of the constant trouble, constant distress, and the passage of time that a pearl is formed. It is not formed in one day. It is distress that creates the pearl, and that is something beautiful that comes out of distress. God gave a prophetic message in an oyster, a low form of life to show us a high form of life.

Our distress creates something beautiful. We are not liberated from our distress, we are given Someone in us, the Holy Spirit, to cover that distress and make it beautiful. He covers our distress and gives glory. He covers the distress of others and brings glory.

And sometimes intercession is constant distress, but something beautiful is produced out of it. Sometimes the burdens we bear for our families, or ourselves or church or country are stressful, and may seem never ending, but they produce something beautiful. In the process we learn to pray, to love, to get God's perspective and people change. Prayer changes people, but prayer also changes us. In that great distress, something beautiful comes out.

Jesus on the cross made intercession. He was the pearl of great price. If you read Isaiah 53, the great chapter in the Old Testament about the sacrifice of Jesus on the cross, it says that He made intercession. His sacrifice absorbed the sin, sorrow and death of the world and released the life of heaven. It was prayer in its highest form. It was a death and life prayer. It was the supreme blood prayer. He poured out His soul for many. It was the sacrifice, the answer to the sacrifice and the intercession through the sacrifice. His terrible distress brought sublime beauty.

Our prayer, like His great prayer, may not be speaking a prayer, but it is blood prayer when we act in a sacrificial way, because it opens the door of heaven for somebody. Blood prayer stands in the gap. Isaiah 53:

> [12]Therefore I will divide Him a portion with the great,
> And He shall divide the spoil with the Strong,
> Because He poured out His soul unto death,

And He was numbered with the transgressors,
And He bore the sin of many,
And made intercession for the transgressors.

The blood is on earth and the blood is in heaven. The blood in heaven, speaks to the blood on earth. All that is out of order on earth, God has put in order in heaven through the cross, so there is blood to blood speaking all the time. The blood of Jesus overcomes the blood of Abel. In other words if you understand this, the blood from heaven stills the cries of the blood, the hurt, the pain, the sickness, the injustice, the disorder and chaos on earth. The blood of Jesus also erases the wages of sin, the bloody mess into which we are born.

The crying and dying of innocent blood started in Genesis, when the blood of Abel cried out after his brother killed him—we go back to the blood. We do not make things right with Cain by beating him up, or paying back the transgressor. The only way that cry of the innocent blood is with the blood of Jesus that has more power.

> [24]to Jesus the Mediator of the new covenant, and to the blood of sprinkling that speaks better things than *that of* Abel. Hebrews 12:24 (NKJV).

Abel's blood cried out and there was no solution, a cry of the innocent, and to some extent, we all have the experience of Abel's blood. There were things that went wrong through no fault of our own. There were things that happened that were not resolved but still hurt. Things that should not have happened, perhaps the cry of a child. But the blood of Jesus has the higher frequency of holiness than the blood of Abel, the cry of innocence. The blood of Jesus calls down all the power of heaven to erase sins, heal hurts, and help the innocent, bring forgiveness and cleansing, breaking through the power of the devil. The blood of Jesus has the transcending power of holiness.

The blood of Abel calls for justice, and the blood of Jesus brings mercy and forgiveness and healing and justice. We cannot always make things right on earth, but the Father, because of the blood, can make things right in heaven. Because of Jesus shedding His blood on earth and taking His blood to heaven and placing that blood on the mercy seat of the temple of God in heaven, the cry of the blood on earth can be resolved and comforted by the blood in heaven. The blood of Jesus settles all scores, for the sinner and the wounded, the guilty and the innocent. How else can this madness and pain end? Intercession is blood to blood, if you want to get down to the absolute core. Those who have standing because of the blood, us, the flesh and blood body of Jesus Christ, washed by the blood of Jesus, can stand in the gap for the blood that is shed and the brokenness and failure of earth. If Jesus had not shed his blood and interceded with his very life, then there would be no power to answer the blood and the innocence and the sins and mistakes that cry out on earth.

So, Christ is continually interceding for the people of God and the world at the right hand of the Father until He returns. Jesus is at the right hand of the Father praying that all that He paid for at the cross becomes a reality on earth. All of redemption and new life, and power and changes in the world, and salvations and healings and deliverances and miracles and family order and marriages and everything under the sun in the will and order of God has been bought and paid for at the cross. When we pray we agree on earth for God's will, and when we pray Jesus has already agreed in heaven for God's will. When He died, He opened a door for God's will to be done on earth as it is in heaven.

Jesus wants to make sure that we don't miss a beat in His blood bought promises and provision and redemption and so He ever lives to make intercession at the Father's right hand to make certain it happens. Jesus bought and paid for the new creation, and undoing the works of the devil. He bought and paid for a choice that we could avoid hell and go to heaven. He is as passionate about making certain his sacrifice is fully realized, just as He was passionate on the cross. "It is finished" is the constant message between heaven and earth through the cross.

Jesus is continually interceding for us, now, from His place in heaven. What He paid for in His death which interceded for us, He is now releasing on the earth realm from heaven to us and through us in His intercession. Jesus is going to be doing that until He returns. We need to do our part too. Even though He has done His part, if we don't do our part in intercession and obedience, His part cannot be released. When He returns it will be a time of judgment and there will be no more interceding for the mercy and grace provided at the cross. That too is finished.

> 24But He, because He continues forever, has an unchangeable priesthood. 25Therefore He is also able to save to the uttermost those who come to God through Him, since He always lives to make intercession for them. Hebrews 7:24 - 25 (NKJV).

He ever lives to do this because He is passionate about saving His creation through His salvation. He loved us enough to create us, to die for us, and He loves us enough to pray that we receive the full measure of redemption. But when the judgments come and the time of the cross is over, then He will not be sitting at the right hand of the Father interceding for anyone, He will be coming on His white horse with the hosts of heaven. The time of intercession will be over and His kingdom will come.

Jesus is able to save to the uttermost. There is no sinner He cannot save. There is no sin He cannot wash away. There is no depth of our souls that He cannot reach. There is no trauma that He cannot erase. There is no death that He cannot reverse. There is no shame that He cannot wash away. There is no old nature that He cannot replace with a new nature. There is no grief that He cannot carry. There is no curse that He cannot break. There is no injustice that He cannot make right and then some. There is no blessing of salvation that He cannot apply. There is no atom or molecule in our body, soul, or spirit that He cannot reach, time backwards, present and future. There is no gift of our lives or our substance that He cannot multiply good measure pressed down, shaken together and running over. He rescues, He delivers. Every person out there that seems to be out of reach, He can save them.

Finally, Romans 8:26 - 27 (NKJV):

> 26Likewise the Spirit also helps in our weaknesses. For we do not know what we should pray for as we

ought, but the Spirit Himself makes intercession £for us
with groanings which cannot be uttered. 27Now He
who searches the hearts knows what the mind of the
Spirit *is*, because He makes intercession for the saints
according to *the will of* God.

We are the body of Christ on earth, and the Holy Spirit is making
intercession through us and for us, according to the will of God. So
not only is Jesus making intercession in heaven to fulfill the will of
the Father and the sacrifice of the Son, but the Holy Spirit is making
intercession on earth to bring it to pass, and are not the angels sent
out as ministers to the heirs of salvation? So there is a working out
of "on earth as it is in heaven." The Holy Spirit has been given to
us, the Spirit of all truth, the Spirit that travails for the mercy and
gifts and love of God to be realized on earth. The Holy Spirit is in
agreement with the will of God the Father in heaven, the intercession
of the Son, and the work of the cross and resurrection to be fully
seen in the earth realm. Hallelujah, what a Savior!

CHAPTER EIGHTEEN

The Butler and the Baker
A Revelation of the Cross

The story of Joseph contains all the themes of Jesus in scripture. The story of Joseph reveals the first coming of Jesus, His cross, burial, resurrection, His second coming, the tribulation and millennial reign, until the new Pharaoh comes, and Satan is loosed. Joseph like Jesus was sold into slavery and wounded by his half-brothers as Jesus would later suffer in fulfillment of Zechariah 13:6. "I was wounded in the house of my friends." Joseph goes through death, and burial, to be resurrected to rule Egypt, second only to Pharaoh, (God the Father). He marries a Gentile bride as our Lord does and is reconciled to his brethren. The parallels between Jesus and Joseph are many.

Joseph is prophetically described as a "fruitful bough" by Jacob, his father. His name in Hebrew means "He will add", given by his mother. Jesus is the Righteous Branch and the One who multiplied the loaves and the fishes and expands the kingdom and inheritance of His Father. Significantly Joseph is given the Egyptian name, "Zaphnathpaaneah", meaning "the one who furnishes the nourishment of life," and "treasury of the glorious rest," as Joseph, with the Spirit of God in him would furnish and nourish life in his brothers and the Egyptians (the world). Jesus said, I am the Bread of Life, He is our Sabbath and Rest, and He is the Lamb of God Who takes away the sin of the world. John 1:29. The story of Joseph itself and the messages of the dreams reveal secrets of the kingdom, the

Messiah, and the coming age. Also, in time, the secrets of guilt and wrongdoing buried in the lives of his brethren are finally revealed. Jesus said, there is nothing hidden that shall not be revealed. The story of Joseph is encoded with the story of Jesus.

The story of Joseph is noteworthy for the importance of dreams. Joseph has two dreams, the butler and baker have one each, and Pharaoh has two dreams. They are all woven into the same fabric of Messianic prophecy. The dreams of the butler and baker are presented in the center of the two sets of repetitive dreams, Joseph's and Pharaoh's, as an axis and a passageway. We will deal with this later. Joseph's dreams of the sheaves and the stars are a continuation and refinement of his great-grandfather Abraham's visions of the stars and the sand of the sea. Although Abraham is the father of faith for the Messiah, Joseph, a chosen descendant, is a prototype of the righteous seed of many, the Bright and Morning Star that shines out of the darkness from many stars.

The sheaves of the field and the stars of the sky show Jesus. In this dream all the sheaves bow to Joseph's sheaf as His works are more righteous that theirs and they will serve him (Him). They don't want to accept his position and glory, and try to get rid of him out of envy, putting him in a pit. In the end His harvest is more upright, as Jesus is Lord of the Harvest, and He is righteousness.

The stars, sun and moon also make obeisance, for He (Jesus) is the Bright and Morning Star. Abraham's vision was that his descendants would be as the stars of the sky. Now one star is brighter, the Messiah's. The vision is carried on through Joseph. He shines brighter than all of his brethren.

Pharaoh's dreams have a prophetic end-time interpretation: The 7 years of fat cattle and fat ears of corn correspond to the first half of the tribulation when all seems well. The 7 lean years with the starving cattle and blasted ears of corn are the second half of the tribulation marked with lack and suffering. Why seven years when the tribulation alone is a 3 1/2 year period in the favorable part and 3 1/2 years in the unfavorable part making a total of 7 years? I believe it is for emphasis, just as God repeats Pharaoh's dream for emphasis. It is because an earthly tribulation for Joseph's brethren will occur twice—in Joseph's time and at the Great Tribulation, the time of Jacob's troubles.

Joseph's brothers do not prepare for the tribulation. They are taken by surprise. It is both a time of judgment and mercy for them. Earthly judgment and divine mercy, as the cross has always stood for those who believe. They must cry to their God, come to Him, humble themselves before Him. Their God has been veiled to their eyes because of their sins and when they repent of their sins He will reveal Himself to them. The affliction of the famine, the potential ruin of their family, and the guilt that they feel regarding their brother, finally causes they to come to the end of themselves and repent. The 7 fat years are the first 3 1/2 years of the tribulation. Joseph's brothers do not realize that famine is coming after this 7 year period. They have stored nothing for the future because they are disconnected from the one who would reveal such secrets to them and who is the source of abundance. When famine does come, they must come to terms with their sin. Judgment has come in adversity and it is then they examine themselves and remember their sin. After they remember their sin, Joseph (Jesus) reveals himself to them and saves their house – in the second half of the tribulation. The tribulation is a time of earthly judgment for the Jews and the world. The church, (or perhaps more specifically the bride) of Jesus Christ, does not experience this judgment. During the time of judgment the brothers will receive revelation of Jesus, as their eye have been blinded to Him and the cross. Unlike the believing Gentiles most of Jesus' natural brethren have not taken their judgment to the cross.

The first part of the second coming as many commentators have interpreted it, is the rapture of the church, prior to the Great Tribulation. The second part is the revelation of Jesus to the Jews. The Book of Revelation is not only the revelation Jesus has as transmitted to the Apostle John, but a revelation by Jesus of Himself to His brethren. The time of revelation is approaching. Yet, prior to the brethren's revelation is the cross. It is God's divine order.

For that reason, in the middle, between the promise of the Messiah to the Jews, the Son of God, and the tribulation when the ultimate man of the flesh is revealed, during which the Jews find their Messiah, stands the dreams of the cross where the man of the flesh dies and then the man of the spirit is resurrected. It is cross from which all things originate because the cross ends all things and the cross begins all things. The cross ends the old man, and begins the new man.

The odd dreams of the butler and baker stand are central to the dreams of Joseph's story. The same Holy Spirit that gave Joseph the interpretation of the butler and baker's dream in Genesis Chapter 40, gave me the interpretation of the interpretation. It is important that Joseph sees his own dreams of power and glory before he interprets the butler and baker's dreams. Jesus, too, for the hope set before Him endured the cross. He saw the glory, but then had to endure the cross. First came the Promise, (promises to Abraham, promises to Joseph, promises to Jesus,) then the cross, then the kingdom. These two relatively mundane dreams, by two prison mates of Joseph, are a key to the other dreams and the key to Joseph's exaltation in the court of Pharaoh.

The wine of the butler and the bread of the baker are the elements of communion. Everywhere that bread and wine appear in scripture, we must ask, why? The next question is, why did the butler live and the baker die? Here is the story of the cross.

To find out why one lives and the other dies, we must decipher the dreams based on scriptural principles. Who are the parties, what are the elements? Pharaoh represents Father God. The Chief Butler, is his chief servant, Jesus. The Chief Butler fills Pharaoh's cup and tastes it first. It is Pharaoh's cup, and the cup Pharaoh has chosen. The baker on the other hand is a man of the flesh, and he gives his baked goods (bread) to Pharaoh.

The dreams of the butler and baker and their fulfillment is a picture of the redemptive work of the cross. These dreams are the axis of two other sets of dreams in the story, Joseph's own two dreams of the sheaves and the stars, and Pharaoh's two dreams of the seven fat and lean years. All six dreams have personal relevance to Joseph and spiritual relevance, as Joseph (Jesus) dreams of the promise of his inheritance, experiences the cross, and then comes again to be part of the rapture, tribulation and revelation of Himself to the world and the Jews.

It is fitting that Joseph should prophetically interpret these dreams foretelling the cross while he was in prison as that was the time of his own death and burial when he cries out to be remembered to Pharaoh. Jesus too preached to those in prison when He went to the underworld. The prophecies were personal to the butler and baker, but also were divinely coded messages to Joseph, as the man of the flesh in Joseph died in prison and man of the spirit rose. Of course, these dreams would be ultimately fulfilled in Jesus Christ as He bore "on the tree" our flesh and curses, but then was exalted to the right hand of the Father, to present His blood.

Joseph would find that the cross is hidden in the fabric of our dreams, and a revelation of the cross is the key to our greatest God-given dreams. The cross is hidden in our dreams and the way out of our most terrible nightmares to our highest hopes.

Genesis 40:

1 And it came to pass after these things, that the butler of the king of Egypt and his baker had offended their lord and king of Egypt.

2 And Pharaoh was wroth against two of his officers, against the chief of the butlers, and against the chief of the bakers.

3 And he put them in ward in the house of the captain of the guard, into the prison, the place where Joseph was bound.

4 And the captain of the guard charged Joseph with them, and he served them: and they continued a season in ward.

5 And they dreamed a dream both of them, each man his dream in one night, each man according to the interpretation of his dream, the butler and the baker of the king of Egypt, which were bound in prison.

6 And Joseph came in unto them in the morning, and looked upon them, and, behold, they were sad.

7 And he asked Pharaoh's officers that were with him in the ward of his lord's house, saying, Wherefore look ye sadly today?

8 And they said unto him, We have dreamed a dream, and there is no interpreter of it. And Joseph said unto them, Do not interpretations belong to God? Tell me them, I pray you.

9 And the chief butler told his dream to Joseph, and said to him, In my dream, behold, a vine was before me;

10 And in the vine were three branches: and it was as though it budded, and her blossoms shot forth; and the clusters thereof brought forth ripe grapes;

11 And Pharaoh's cup was in my hand: and I took the grapes, and pressed them into Pharaoh's cup, and I gave the cup into Pharaoh's hand.

12 And Joseph said unto him, This is the interpretation of it: The tree branches are three days;

13 Yet within three days shall Pharaoh lift up thine head, and restore thee unto thy place; and thou shalt deliver Pharaoh's cup into his hand, after the former manner when thou wast his butler.

14 But think on me when it shall be well with thee, and shew kindness, I pray thee, unto me, and make mention of me unto Pharaoh, and bring me out of this house.

15 For indeed I was stolen away out of the land of the Hebrews; and here also have I done nothing that they should put me into the dungeon.

16 When the chief baker saw that the interpretation was good, he said unto Joseph, I also was in my dream, and, behold, I had three white baskets on my head:

17 And in the uppermost basket there was of all

manner of bakemeats for Pharaoh; and the birds did eat them out of the basket upon my head.

18 And Joseph answered and said, This is the interpretation thereof: The three baskets are three days:

19 Yet within three days shall Pharaoh lift up thy head from off thee, and shall hang thee on a tree; and the birds shall eat thy flesh from off thee.

20 And it came to pass the third day, which was Pharaoh's birthday, that he made a feast unto all his servants; and he lifted up the head of the chief butler and of the chief baker among his servants.

21 And he restored the chief butler unto his butlership again; and he gave the cup into Pharaoh's hand:

22 But he hanged the chief baker: as Joseph had interpreted to them.

23 Yet did not the chief butler remember Joseph, but forgat him.

It is significant that the butler and baker say, "We have dreamed a dream" in verse 8 of the King James Version. Just as Joseph's dreams are one in the same and Pharaoh's dreams are one in the same, so too the butler and baker's dreams are one in the same, two sides of one message. It is one message delivered by two dreams. It is important that two people have one message because two spiritual "men," one of the flesh and one of the spirit, incorporate one message in these dreams and Pharaoh decrees judgment or mercy on their lives.

The chief butler tells his dream to Joseph, verses 9 - 11. The vine is before him. He sees three branches that bud and produce grapes. The chief butler personally takes the cluster of grapes and squeezes them, producing juice, into Pharaoh's cup which is in his hand at the fulfilled third day. In interpretation of it, Joseph states the three branches are three days, and in three days the chief butler would be lifted up to his former position (Pharaoh would lift up thy head) at the right hand of Pharaoh. Joseph says remember me. "I have done nothing wrong."

On the other hand, the baker sees three white baskets on his head in his dream. The birds eat from the top basket. Joseph interprets the bakers dream to the effect that in three days he would be "hung on a tree" and the birds "shall eat thy flesh".

The chief butler and baker describe the work of Jesus on the cross. Wine represents the "blood" in the communion, and bread represents the "body." Jesus is both divine and human. It is His divine blood, the Father's blood, that makes Him the Son of God. It is His flesh that makes Him the Son of Man. That which is divine does not perish with Jesus. It is not judged, but He bears the judgment of the world in the flesh, because the flesh must be judged and die.

The chief butler represents the spirit man, the Son of God. Jesus, as the butler, holds grapes in His hand that have taken three days to ripen. So too with Jesus the maturation of His work at the cross will take three days. It is then He presents His blood to the Father. Like the butler squeezing the ripe grapes into Pharaoh's cup Jesus has squeezed out His own life. No one else has done it because He allows His death as it says in John 10:18. He has the authority to lay down His life and the authority to raise it up. These are chosen grapes as Jesus' blood is chosen blood, divine blood. Jesus is given the cup by the Father, the cup of suffering, the cross. He does not select this cup; He takes it as a servant and there He pours His life into the cup in death. He is the first to taste of the cup because He tastes death for all humankind, and makes priestly intercession for all men and women back to the Father and through His blood gives access to all to the Father. Then He presents the cup of His completed work, His shed blood, back to the Father, where it is placed on the mercy seat. After the cross Jesus is seated together at the right hand of the Father. His "head is lifted up" because the authority, dominion, and power of that Head is restored to its proper place at the right hand of the Father.

The butler, the wine bearer lives, as the divine Son of God has the power of an endless life. The blood ever lives on the mercy seat to erase our sin. It does not putrefy, as it is divine holy blood.

The Father receives the blood and will not reject the blood because it is the divine part of Jesus, His supernatural inheritance as the Son of God. It is pure and holy and the blood cleanses us from sin. It is the mercy of God which flows from the cross to the mercy seat of heaven.

The baker on the other hand is "hung on a tree" like Jesus, representing the body of Jesus, His earthly part. Because of sin, the flesh must die. We know that no flesh can see God and live—only resurrected flesh can come into the presence of God.

The Father rejects the body as it is contaminated and must die. It bears our sin, sickness, self, the three white baskets, which culminate in death. Jesus on the cross bears our sin and sickness, and dies to self experiencing the conclusion of all these things for us. At the cross He dies, and we die, so we may be reborn and experience His resurrection. I believe the topmost basket is "self" as the man of the flesh exalts self and exaltation of self is the source from which sin, sickness and death flow. Exaltation of self, the god of self, is the door for evil spirits (the birds) to gain access to man, just as when Jesus is exalted, there is an open door for the Holy Spirit's access.

It is interesting that the cross should be revealed in Egypt, where the Passover is initiated and Jesus will also live for a season fleeing from Herod, in fulfillment of the prophecy, "I called my son out of Egypt." Hosea 11:1. These deep seeds of revelation were planted in the dreams of Pharaoh's servants.

The cross holds both mercy and judgment, mercy for our sins through the blood, judgment to the flesh as it is killed and carries the old nature to the grave. We are dead to the flesh, but alive to God. But the cross also presents the larger picture of judgment, we will either judge ourselves at the cross or be judged by it. As stated, the butler's grapes are squeezed into the cup, and presented to the Father (Pharaoh) after three days: Genesis 40:10:

> And in the vine *were* three branches: and it *was as*
> though it budded, *and* her blossoms shot forth; and
> the clusters thereof brought forth ripe grapes.

The butler himself, who serves Pharaoh, sees and performs this process just as Jesus Himself presents the blood to the Father. The grapes are selected by hand and pressed by hand when Jesus Himself offers Himself to death to fill that cup at the cross.

On the other hand, in the book of Revelation, we see the winepress of the wrath of God, because the blood of Jesus has been rejected by an unbelieving world. These grapes are trampled by foot, the end result of trampling on the blood of Jesus and rejecting it. These grapes are indiscriminate; all feel the judgment, whatever the degree of guilt or innocence.

The blood of Jesus is chosen fruit. The blood of others is indiscriminate.

Blood of Mercy, Blood of Judgment

The grapes of love are squeezed out by hand,

They have reached perfection and righteously stand.

The blood of Jesus is presented in our election

If we accept His divine correction,

Partake in His death, His blood, His resurrection.

The grapes of wrath await His rejection,

They are trampled by foot without selection.

Blood of judgment, blood of execution,

To purge the earth of its defection.

On the other hand the baker represents the flesh dying on the cross. We know the bread comes from the seed. Every seed dies in the earth, produces more seed in the harvest, which are broken, crushed, mixed with oil, sometimes mixed with leaven, cooked and eaten. Bread carries leaven which represents sin.

The grape on the other hand is squeezed and the pulp is emptied, but the blood is not dead. It is transformed into wine, holy wine.

On His body, Jesus bore the judgment of all flesh on the cross. His body died because it carried our judgment and death. The birds, (evil spirits) pick at the baker's body, as evil spirits have access to unregenerate flesh which is cursed. The Bible says, cursed is everyone who hangs on a tree. The forces of evil torment and brutalize and murder the flesh of Jesus, as He bore our condemnation in the flesh.

However, evil spirits cannot touch the blood because it is not hanged on a tree, or cursed, but poured out. It does not bear our sins but erases them.

As the scripture states, the baker's head is "lifted off" of him. Human flesh is judged and dethroned for all time at the cross. The works of the baker's hands cannot please Pharaoh, because the works of the flesh do not fulfill righteousness or judgment, just as Cain's fruits were not an acceptable sacrifice to God. God could not accept Cain's sacrifice because it stood in opposition to the blood of His Son, and if accepted, would make the blood of Christ of none effect. The three baskets are on the baker's head show the baker himself "exalts his works," but they do not sanctify the head of the baker and are not acceptable. The baskets are "white" and seem pure, but their white outward appearance do not mask the works of the flesh, as they are made by hand, and contain works of his hand.

Both body and blood are imprisoned, but the blood goes to the mercy seat (up) and the body goes down to the grave (down).

In verse 14, Joseph tells the chief butler to remember him to Pharaoh to "bring me out of this house." This statement resonates with spiritual meaning as Jesus cries on the cross, "My God, My God, why hast thou forsaken me." Jesus cries to be remembered to His Father. The thief at the cross cries "Remember me". Further, the blood is shed to "remember" mankind to the Father, lost in the dungeon of sin. Finally, at that final Passover feast recorded for all generations, His Last Supper, Jesus says, "Remember Me" to His disciples. Our Lord cries out to be remembered in the hearts of men and women for whom He died on the cross, for what He did on the cross. Jesus cries to be remembered to God. Man cries to be remembered to God. Jesus asks to be remembered to man. All parties seek reconciliation and remembrance.

God hates divorce, as He was the first to experience it when His creation decided upon its own course, rejected His love and became unfaithful. At the cross there is reconciliation for the world, and at the revelation of Jesus, reconciliation for the Jews. God has been standing in faith a long time for this reconciliation. Jesus the Bridegroom waits in the final moments of this age for His bride. The blood covenant took place at the cross.

In verse 15 Joseph protests his innocence. "I have done nothing that they should put me into the dungeon," just as Jesus was innocently put to death. I Peter 3:17-22 sum up the story of the butler and baker.

> 17 For it is better, if the will of God be so, that ye suffer for well doing, than for evil doing.
>
> 18 For Christ also hath once suffered for sins, the just for the unjust, that He might bring us to God, being put to death in the flesh, but quickened by the Spirit:
>
> 19 By which also He went and preached unto the spirits in prison;
>
> 20 Which sometime were disobedient, when once the long suffering of God waited in the days of Noah, while the ark was a preparing, wherein few, that is, eight souls were saved by water.
>
> 21 The like figure whereunto even baptism doth also now save us (not the putting away of the filth of the flesh, but the answer of a good conscience toward God) by the resurrection of Jesus Christ:
>
> 22 Who is gone into heaven, and is on the right hand of God; angels and authorities and powers being made subject unto Him.

The story of Joseph is the story of promise, death, exaltation and fulfillment. Let us look to Jesus, the Author and Finisher of our faith and the Great Revelator. All six dreams of the story of Joseph have one message and fulfillment: Jesus Christ the same yesterday, today and forever. There would be more to come. After the cross comes the time of judgment, but for now, we live in the grace and (anointing) shadow of the cross.

Jesus, states in Revelation 1:8: "I am Alpha and Omega, the beginning and the ending... which is, and which was and which is to come, the Almighty." He is here today to pour out that same Spirit of revelation on all flesh that the seeds planted in the scripture might grow and bring forth the harvest of the kingdom through the cross.

Part III

The Destination of the Cross

CHAPTER NINETEEN

It Is Finished

When Jesus therefore had received the vinegar, He said, "It is finished,"and He bowed His head, and gave up the ghost. John 20:30.

Behold, I come as a thief. Blessed is he that watcheth, and keepeth his garments, lest he walk naked, and they see his shame. And he gathered them together into a place called in the Hebrew tongue Armageddon. And the seventh angel poured out his vial into the air, and there came a great voice out of the temple of heaven, from the throne, saying, "It is done." And there were voices and thunders, and lightnings; and there was a great earthquake, such was not since men were upon the earth, so mighty an earthquake, and so great. And the great city was divided into three parts, and the cities of the nations fell: and great Babylon came in remembrance before God, to give unto her the cup of the wine of the fierceness of His wrath. Revelation 16:15-19.

Before the fall God created and He rested. His completion of creation was at the end of the sixth day, and He saw that it was not only good, but very good with the creation of man and woman. It was completed: The finished work of creation was done.

But at the fall, the universe was reversed, and creation lost its connection to God. It was corrupted, interrupted, disturbed, and chaotic without His hand and order. That is why,

> ...the earnest expectation of the creature waits for the manifestation of the sons of God... because the creature itself also shall be delivered form the bondage of corruption into the glorious liberty of the children of God. For we know that the whole creation groans and travails in pain together until now. Romans 8:19, 21-22.

Creation waits for the manifestation of the sons of God, and the manifestation of the Son of God, to be put out of its misery, disorder, and corruption. We all groan waiting for that day.

We know that the cross was God's method to restore fallen creation—the sublime plan of love that could only originate from the Creator. At the cross God proved He would never leave us nor forsake us. There creation was finished again in its deformed state and started again in its reformed place, for the cross equals love and love equals the cross. It is the divine equation for all new beginnings, *and the definer of the divine. As I have written, everything ends and begins at the cross; it ends the old creation and begins the new.*

Here we come to the story of two judgments, two cups, two wraths, two endings to creation's story. Choose.

Jesus said, *It is finished.* The finished work of His death on the cross is the act of undoing the works of the devil. "For this purpose the Son of God was manifested, that He might destroy the works of the devil." I John 3:8. It was the divine work of the Father, Son and Holy Spirit to break the power of hell over the planet. The Father gave all, the Son gave all, and the Holy Spirit gave all. *Heaven waged everything on the cross.*

First the Father gave all: He gave His only begotten Son. Jesus was the only Son physically born of God the Father, the Father's only Child. Jesus Christ was the Father's only hope of carrying on His nature in creation and of leaving His inheritance to a lost world, replacing the DNA of death, with the DNA of eternal life. Furthermore, the Father loved the Son.

If the gift of His Son failed, if the Son had sinned like Adam and forsaken righteousness, if He had not stayed on the cross, but called the angels to His rescue, don't you know, *HEAVEN AND EARTH WOULD HAVE COLLAPSED!* Heaven would have lost Jesus and earth would have lost heaven. God the Son would have ceased being who He is and was, the Word itself, and all that the Word upheld would have crashed. Creation would have terminated, and the power of God eliminated in the earth realm. We would never have entrance into the kingdom of heaven, but would have been lost in darkness forever, left in torment for eternity. The Father risked it all, even risked losing His beloved Son. He risked darkness over the universe forever.

The Son staked everything on His trust of the Father. He trusted Himself to the will of the Father, even when He couldn't see Him, hear Him, or fellowship with Him; even when He was rejected of the Father; even in agony; even as He carried the sins of the world, died, and was wrapped in a cloth and placed in a grave, sealed with a stone—He trusted His Father.

Third, the Spirit waged everything on the obedience of the Son and the plans of the Father in the strategy of the cross. If the cross had failed in its work, Jesus in His travail and intercession, there would be no new creation through which the Spirit could express the will of the Father in the sons and daughters of God.

Finally, the Father and the Son entrusted themselves to the Eternal Spirit, who accomplished the first great creation, and was now commissioned to empower the cross, the resurrection, the birthing of sons and daughters of God, and the church.

But we know with certainty that God, the Father, the Son and the Holy Spirit, didn't fail, and the cross did prevail.

<u>How can we can unequivocally state this? How do we know? We know this because love never fails and God is love and love is God, and in this was the love of God manifest, that God gave His only begotten Son to be the propitiation (substitute sacrifice) for our sins.</u>

We know this because the Word never fails, and no word of God will ever fall to the ground and die, not to be resurrected and bring forth its promised increase, certainly not the Word of the Son. We know this because He said it would happen in the way it did, and because the law and the prophets told of His suffering.

He took the judgment, He took the cup of wrath, He became the supper for us. He gave His body and blood, so that we could be pulled over the "It is Finished" line.

At the cross Jesus said, it is finished. What was finished? One thing that was finished were the works of the devil. He broke the power of rebellion that originated in the throne room of heaven, then trashed creation, and finally disabled and perverted man and woman's image, anointing, identity, power and authority. Because of the cross, the curse on the earth will eventually be broken. At the cross it was finished, reversed, disassembled, torn down. He gave us His Person, power, purpose, plan, position, possession, and promises to continue the work. He gave us the keys of the kingdom.

It is finished: We can choose the cross, and there all scores are settled, enemies forgiven, grudges dropped, wounds healed, sins forgiven, sinners released, and demons and sicknesses overcome. Our mothers, fathers, sisters, brothers, friends, betrayers, lovers, haters, are liberated from every tie, lie, definition, distortion, creation that is not based on the blood of Jesus, and the finished work of the cross. The bondages, curses, and patterns of sin for generations are broken, and the false image that we have proudly worn, laid down, like a dirty garment.

The war in our hearts is finished, the war with heaven is finished, and the war on earth is finished, for there is peace on earth by the blood of the cross. There has been no conflict through the ages that did not originate in our hearts, and it must end. The life-love blood of Jesus speaks louder than blood of Abel.

At the cross we can judge ourselves and turn aside the judgment of heaven because He took it. We have sinned against heaven and in the sight of others, and if we will but repent, that judgment will be ended. He carried it, He buried it, and He ended it, He defended it in His resurrection. It is finished. We do not have to work out our salvation through our own sweat and blood, but work out our salvation through His sweat and blood. He trades His righteousness for our trash, and releases the love and truth to cleanse and restore a planet.

But someday the world will no longer be able to avail itself of the communion, the broken body and blood, the divine declaration of love sealed with, "It is finished."

The question of the hour, each hour, is, "Which supper will you choose?" The supper of the cross where our flesh dies, and we can commune again with heaven on earth, or the supper of judgment, where our flesh rots, and the end game of heaven's wrath is finally poured on earth's rebellion. Keep the flesh and it will be judged, judge the flesh and you will be freed. The flesh is judged. The choice is whether we do the judging, or the judging is done by the judgments on the earth and at the judgment seat of God.

Here is the supper of the Great God: "The fowls of the air will be gathered to the supper of the great God, to eat the flesh of kings, captains, mighty men, horses, ...and the flesh of all men, both small and great..." in judgement. Revelation 19:17-18. After the seventh vial of judgment is poured, a voice out of the Temple of heaven from the throne will say, "It is done," rather than "it is finished." Revelation 16:17. God finally had to put an end the rebellion of this planet in judgment—it is done. There is a supper, but it is a supper of judgment on the flesh. He has given divine grace. His heart has been expanded and stretched beyond anything in the universe with the death of His Son, but eventually He must close the door.

And so the choice of judgment or mercy is given to us all, between a man on a cross who carries our judgment, or rejection of a cross to experience our judgment. Either way, God will purge this planet. Either way, blood is shed. The question is, will it be the blood of Jesus, or ours? Will we be plunged in the stream of His blood, by our choice, to end sin and us, or we will be plunged in our own blood, by His choice, to end sin and us.

Today the choice is still yours and mine. Oh how He loves us and how much He wants to take the judgment from us. Choose.

CHAPTER TWENTY

Communion for the World
The Message and Exhortation
of the Cross

This is where I want to take you, where God is leading me to have the cross burned in your heart. Psalms 23:5-6:

> 5Thou preparest a table before me in the presence of mine enemies: thou anointeth my head with oil; my cup runneth over. 6 Surely goodness and mercy shall follow me all the days of my life: and I will dwell in the house of the LORD forever.

> Your beauty and love chase after me every day of my life. I'm back home in the house of God for the rest of my life. Psalms 23:6 (TMSG).

Bread and wine, body and blood, communion, reunion, God's tokens of love. And here is how it happened. Christmas tells the story of a divine birth, which is birthed in our hearts, but Christmas also points the way to a divine death and resurrection. Both are breathtaking. Jesus came humbly, He lived humbly, He died humbly, but He rose gloriously, and will come back as King. All our births carry the story of the wages of sin and death, our cells, DNA, emotional histories, are contaminated, but Jesus interrupted the pattern—He did not carry the wages of sin and death, but He carried the gift of God, so that we could be gifts of God. That is the gift that keeps on giving. In every step we take, the sacrifice is there, the price has been paid for freedom, for the power of God, for the grace of God, for the love of God. David desired to move the ark of the covenant to Jerusalem so that the presence of God could dwell there and bless the whole nation. II Samuel 6. As the priests carried the ark, David danced before the Lord and made a sacrifice to the Lord every six paces. Six paces, sacrifice. Six paces, sacrifice. It was a long and bloody journey to Jerusalem. But in the same way, it was going to take a sacrifice to move us into the presence of God, and to move us forward in the kingdom, which is just what the Lord did—Who for the joy set before Him endured the cross.

Jesus was conceived by the Holy Spirit, empowered by and led by the Holy Spirit. He was the divine example of how God was repairing and restoring the earth. He was love in the flesh, God in the flesh. The greatest fulfillment of this was the divine death, that cleanses the world from its sin, and the divine life in the resurrection that propels us to new life, supernatural life, abundant life.

You and I can stop the wages of sin, any time, but it takes a change of heart by receiving the gift of God, day by day, and working out our own salvation with fear and trembling. You can stop the power of the enemy, but it takes facing the enemy within. Most of our enemies are within. We only can prosper as our souls prosper, it says 3 John 2. We are born into sin and condemnation, but we are born again in righteousness so we partake of this holy time, every month, and prepare our hearts.

> God rewrote the text of my life when I opened the book of my heart to his eyes. Here is a time we can open the book of our hearts to God. God rewrote it. It is changed because I opened the book of my heart. 2 Samuel 22:25 (TMSG).

We come to the communion table. It is a table of common unity. Communion is a time of fellowship, with God and each other. We come to partake of our God and we come together to share this with each other. We enter into a blood covenant with the Lord, the everlasting covenant, and actually a blood covenant with each other as brothers and sisters. It is very holy and very solemn, because what binds us is the holy blood of Jesus. The holy blood interrupts the unholy blood and changes our destiny.

This is not a laughing and light Christianity, it is a blood and guts Christianity where Jesus was willing to experience pain and suffering we cannot imagine to deliver God's love to us. It is a meal we all share and must share. And folks, we are forced to share it with each other so that we will examine ourselves. Communion means common unity, unity with God and each other. I John 1:7 tells us,

> If we walk in the light as He is in the light we have fellowship one with another (Father, Son, Holy Spirit and the body of Christ) and the blood of Jesus Christ cleanses us from all sin.

The Old Testament says, you shall not hate your brother in your heart. If you are angry, then express your anger and go on. Leviticus 19:17 - 18:

> [17]Thou shalt not hate thy brother in thine heart: thou shalt in any wise rebuke thy neighbour, and not suffer sin upon him. [18]Thou shalt not avenge, nor bear any grudge against the children of thy people, but thou shalt love thy neighbour as thyself: I *am* the LORD.

Communion is a time to let go of things at the cross, which we have against others, and cling onto the benefits of our salvation. John 17:11 says,

> And now I am no more in the world, but these are in the world, and I come to thee. Holy Father, keep through thine own name those whom thou hast given me, that they may be one, as we *are*.

Our table is truly a table set in the presence of our enemies, for we are called out of the world to eat the feast that the Lord has prepared for us. In the middle of the wilderness of this world, God has prepared something for us. God has prepared something for us! We may experience hardship or emptiness or loss in life, but the feast is there, and we have abundance more than we understand. This feast is there to remind us where we got the abundance, and where we go for abundance. Our God is our source and our Lord. We have enemy attacks, but the feast is there to renew and empower us. We live in the world, but are not of the world, for what feeds us is heavenly, not earthly. Our feast is heavenly food. We must be determined to live by heavenly values, heavenly nourishment, heavenly direction, and heavenly love.

At the cross, all the blood of the Son was poured to the ground, as a drink offering, the cup of suffering, so that we could experience, the cup of communion, the cup of life, and the outpouring of the Holy Spirit. That living blood on earth speaks to the living blood on the mercy seat in heaven.

The cross is for people who really want answers—many believers do not—they are happy to have their lives as it is, happy to compromise, not everyone wants the prize of the high calling, or they want the prize without the price. As we enter into communion, we are supposed to go deep. God Himself had to be divided so we could be put back together again. The cross is our true measure of life and self. It is the place of ultimate truth. A lot of people prize happiness over holiness, but God prizes holiness over happiness. That is the cost of the cross. The cross brings us happy, after holy. Then, as we come into deeper communion with Him, and the old life dies, we see the glory of the new life. The old life is like a seed planted in the ground. It has potential, but only when it dies and brings the beauty and glory that God desires, what He has put in the seed.

People need this, but generally people want what they don't need and need what they don't want. So God in His mercy, takes our hearts and molds us, and changes us, to want what He wants, in the image of His Son. Divine submission is first, then the divine commission. That is God's order.

The power of the body and blood: We know the bread represents the broken body of Christ, which can heal to the uttermost. There is no healing, no life, no restoration, it cannot provide. If you need healing for the deepest part of the cells of your body, the Bread of Life is there. If you need healing for your mind, the Bread is there. He is the Bread of Life. He doesn't just give us something we can hold or feel, He gives Himself. If you are just hungry for life, the Bread is there. He said that He would give life and give it more abundantly—but on His terms. Don't despair on the empty food of the world. It is here and then it is gone, and it is not really living.

And then the blood, which can cleanse to the uttermost, and gives us access to the very throne room of God through the Holy of Holies. If you want your sins washed away, the blood is there. If you want protection, the blood is there. If you want a new and renewed mind instead of a dark and shallow one, the blood is there. It has the power to renew and rewire our thinking and emotional life and history. This is something we must seek and pursue. If your way of life or habits, or depression or sorrow, or circumstances are not what God has promised, or what appears in His word, whether we like it or not, they will cause pain, and the pain is a great motivator. But we are given the opportunity through the pain to seek His will and His way, His healing and deliverance from pain.

You see whenever there is sin, there is the shedding of blood to take care of that sin, and Jesus did it once and for all. Wherever sin is, there is an open door for the enemy. If you want to get out of a pattern of living that is not of God, then go to the cross, because the blood will give you power, and the body will heal those parts of our souls that need healing. You can't do it on your own.

Covenant has been broken, between somebody: Between us and God, and us and ourselves, and us and our neighbors, and us and our family. Covenant was broken the times we were abandoned and rejected, by those who should have stayed, and those who should have loved, but covenant can be renewed by the blood. The blood of the breaking of covenant cries out, but the blood of Jesus cries out even more and can cleanse our hearts. Malachi 4:

> 5Behold, I will send you Elijah the prophet before
> the coming of the great and dreadful day of the

LORD: ⁶And he shall turn the heart of the fathers to the children, and the heart of the children to their fathers, lest I come and smite the earth with a curse.

We are also the children of God and our hearts must be turned to our Father God.

Jesus said, *My body is meat indeed.* Every one of us has a hunger of the soul. Every one of us has pieces missing of our completeness. This bread completes us and fills the hunger. John 6:55 - 57 (NLT):

⁵⁵For my flesh is the true food, and my blood is the true drink. ⁵⁶All who eat my flesh and drink my blood remain in me, and I in them. ⁵⁷I live by the power of the living Father who sent me; in the same way, those who partake of me will live because of me.

The fullness of the body and blood: This body and blood are food for our journey to heaven. This is the food we need and food we crave. By it we are filled, healed, restored to fellowship with God and each other. And by it we are cleansed, forgiven and have the power to forgive others. His body and blood is the meal we need to continue on our journey on earth to heaven. In this journey there are strenuous paths, hard climbs, very difficult decisions, steps of faith, and the power of the body and blood is supernatural food for the journey. Sometimes those difficult decisions are to separate us from that which we have been joined to for a while. Sometimes we need a change of heart, so we can walk a new path, even though we have fear, or face persecution, even though we want to be safe and accepted. It is a difficult path that requires holy food or we cannot and will not make the climb. The high altitude and the path requires us to leave aside the weights and sins that so easily beset us. Steps of faith, are just that, we need faith to take the steps, but that means we must know our Lord—communion with His body and blood.

The body and the blood are the only elements that provide the strength to be released from human flesh and blood. The Bible tells us that flesh and blood shall not inherit the kingdom. Now that is very important concept to break this down.

Let's think about the flesh for a minute. The flesh is strong. It has a will of its own. The flesh has its own desires and motives and lusts and memories. The flesh represents our nature which is not under the control of the Holy Spirit. Flesh will push you to what you desire.

> For he that soweth to his flesh shall of the flesh reap corruption; but he that soweth to the Spirit shall of the Spirit reap life everlasting. Galatians 6:8.

> And they that are Christ's have crucified the flesh with the affections and lusts. Galatians 5:24.

> But God forbid that I should glory, save in the cross of our Lord Jesus Christ, by whom the world is crucified unto me, and I unto the world. Galatians 6:14.

But blood is strong too. It is our ties, our people, our generational curses or blessings. It is what we owe, and what we have inherited and who has experienced the same basic life experiences with us. And blood will push you to do what you don't want to do.

That is why flesh and blood cannot inherit the kingdom.

What is God's solution? We die daily. Our flesh is crucified to the world. And the blood is purified by the blood of Jesus; we have new blood. We overcome the world, flesh and devil by the blood of the Lamb, the word of our testimony and importantly, we love not our lives unto death. Revelation 12:11. That is we place Christ first in all things, because He is first. This is the power of the cross in our communion.

Taking these symbolic elements causes us to remember Him (once a month, or perhaps every day) and what He has done, but our communion is every day, every moment, we are part of His body, we have been adopted by His blood.

You cannot walk the heavenly journey without the body and the blood. This meal fills us with true food, true life, true blessings, true healing, and true power, and we do not need to cave in to the world, the flesh, or the devil. It is our table and a heavenly feast. We have heavenly food for a heavenly future, but also it is the food of heavenly beings in the middle of an evil world. You cannot walk the journey of true life with bad food and empty calories. There is a lot of bad food out there, but it addicts, it gives no strength; it makes us big, but not strong. It is a lie and it breaks down our souls just as it breaks down the cells of our bodies. It is bad food because disobedience always looks pretty and powerful and something that will make us wise and is good to eat, but it is not from the tree of life. It is seductive and corrupting, just as bad food is. It is bad food and not meant for human consumption. Lies are not meant for human consumption—they make us less than what God created us to be. They are from hell. Remember that when the enemy tempts you, it is a spirit from hell that is trying to pass bad food to you, and it is a lie. This is food for demons. Yet, people live their chosen lies anyway, and are destroyed by them, and pass that destruction on to other generations. Jesus says, "My body is food indeed and My blood is drink indeed." The truth from above is for human consumption.

When the children of Israel ate manna, it says in the Bible that they ate angels' food. When the people of God have communion, we have Jesus' body, divine food.

Our table is food for the journey. It strengthens us, for because of its power, by His stripes we are healed. We are given heavenly food, daily bread as often as we take it. Jesus said, I am the Bread of Life. Your fathers ate manna in the wilderness and are dead. He that eats of this bread will never die.

Next it gives is power over all the power of the enemy. It is the table in the presence of our enemies. We live in this world in the presence of our enemies, for our enemies are the enemies of God. Thieves come to steal, kill and destroy. Wolves in sheep's clothing come to scatter God's people. Our own emotions often take us a direction that is outside of the word and will of God. The enemy roars at us and comes to devour, but the hedge of protection of our God is around us. But he cannot come near—he cannot overwhelm our souls. It is because the blood is on us.

When Jesus is in the boat, it does not tip over. When a demonized man runs at Him, the power of the anointing stops the demons.

When the enemy comes in, the Spirit of the Lord raises a standard, the flood of the blood. When God fights for Israel, the sun stands still at the request of a man in one dispensation, and in another, God so loves the world the sun hides its face, and the Son of God shines in unsurpassed love to cover us with His blood. The blood covers us and the blood keeps us from the angel of death. If God be for us, who can be against us?

This is a victory table. All the spoils of the war between God and Satan have been bought by the body and blood. We get back our names, our identities, the truth about our lives, a heavenly home, victory over this world. The devil and sin and sickness and hell and the flesh were defeated there, and abundant, eternal, supernatural and resurrection life are gained there.

Yet, we live in the world. We look at the other person's table. Oh, they have steak over there. They don't look hungry—but we feel empty and lonely at times. They are having lobster, and cheese cake and all the wine and desserts and food they would ever want, plus entertainment, and we look at our little portion of bread and wine. It seems tiny, it seems like a little portion. Sometimes people eat the bread and wine, but are not satisfied, that is because they don't know what it contains, what it costs and what it can do. That little portion is the whole story of God's love on earth. It is all of God which enters into all of us. THAT LITTLE PORTION IS BIGGER THAN ALL THE EARTH AND THE HEAVENS. If you move from this table to the other table you will miss God. That little portion is our inheritance. It is our portion. David writes that the Lord is my portion. Psalms 16:5 (NKJV): *5O Lord, You are the portion of my inheritance and my cup; You maintain my lot.* The Lord was the portion of the children of Israel, and the people of God.

He is what we have in this world. This table is what we have in this world, instead of the world having us. You can gain the whole world and lose your soul. He is the pearl of great price. This table is salvation. Our food for our souls doesn't have to be big and showy and sloppy and overwhelming and gorge our souls, because our table is so absolute. It is tight and neat and final and you can't add anything too it, and you can't subtract anything from it. You can't add cheese and hotdogs and cake to this meal, it would defile it—

you can't add any old crazy thought—Jesus made it simple so you wouldn't miss it; and you can't take away from it, or it would lose its power. Our food for the soul is the Bread of Life. You can't add jam and peanut butter to the Bread of Life. He says, this is My body and this is My blood. Eat it. Drink it. Period.

God set out the pattern and you can't add or subtract from God. That goes for everything in the Bible, and this table is the seed of the whole word, wisdom, and power of God. It represents the love and power and truth of God. It is nothing to be played with. You cannot add to the word of God, you cannot add to the cross, you cannot add to the resurrection, you cannot add to the Holy Spirit, you cannot add or subtract from the love of God, you cannot add your likes and dislikes, what you want to obey and what you don't. You can't add to the blood. You can't add to Jesus. That is true of our lives, you can't add to the word of God, or it will be contaminated and you can't subtract from the word of God or the love of God, or it was be incomplete. You can't add to the love of God anymore than you can add to God.

The first communion is recorded in the book of Genesis when the priest Melchisedek brought bread and wine to Abraham, and the pattern continues through the Bible when the great High Priest Jesus had the last supper with His disciples and said this is My body which is broken for you and this is My blood which is shed for you.

Our table is like the five smooth stones that David shot at Goliath. It is small, but effective, because the anointing is behind it to defeat the enemy. David didn't need artillery. He just needed one smooth stone to stick into the brain of Goliath. Jesus did the same when He crushed the head of the serpent by shedding His blood. One word under the anointing is better than ten thousand sloppy words.

Our table is the feast of kings, and it is where kings are fed and how they are created and it was given by a King. Daniel and his friends Shadrach, Meshach and Abednego, refused the food of the king of Babylon, because it was defiled food, food offered to idols, and ate instead a small diet of vegetables. Even though their names had been changed and bodies probably mutilated, their souls and spirits stayed with the God of Israel. At the end of the appointed time they were stronger and wiser than all the other young men on the king's diet. They were more built up and their minds were prepared to take dominion in the kingdom of Babylon, which represents the world's system. Time and time again, Daniel, a picture of Jesus, was elevated to ruler-ship over all the satanic powers in that province, because they decided that the meal of God was stronger and better than the meal of the world.

The foolishness of God is stronger and wiser than the wisdom of the world. The things that are nothing, because they are of God, are something and the somethings of this world are nothing. The first shall be last and the last shall be first. People look at our table and think, how dumb you are; why are you just eating that tiny little bit of food when you could have everything in the world. But they do not understand. <u>The cross is foolish, but the cross has power. The meal seems small, but the food is really gigantic. It is the food of overcomers, conquerors, kings and priests and sons and daughters of God.</u>

Love not the world, neither the things that are of the world, for he that loves the world does not love the Father. 1 John 2:15 - 17 (TMSG):

> [15]Don't love the world's ways. Don't love the world's goods. Love of the world squeezes out love for the Father. [16]Practically everything that goes on in the world—wanting your own way, wanting everything for yourself, wanting to appear important—has nothing to do with the Father. It just isolates you from him. [17]The world and all its wanting, wanting, wanting is on the way out—but whoever does what God wants is set for eternity.

It is a table that is costly: Our communion table is the costliest meal ever prepared, and we are invited to it whenever we want to go. It is so humble that people all over the world eat it, poor people, rich people, it is the same meal for everyone, and it gives them the same power of an overcoming life. God gave us a table that everyone could afford because it was so lowly, and no one could afford it, no matter how rich they were, because it was so costly. No one's communion table is better or richer, because we all take of this humble piece of bread and this little bit of juice. We are all redeemed at the same cost, the precious blood of Jesus.

The book of Song of Solomon is read at Passover. Now if you have read your Bible, you know that the Song of Solomon is a love story and a pretty erotic one at that. It seems like a romance in the middle of the Bible, but it is God romancing His people. Passover on the other hand is the story of Israel leaving Egypt, and the killing of a lamb and the putting of blood over the house so the angel of death would not kill the people of Israel. Passover points to the death of Christ. It seems like an odd combination, to read a love story at the bloody time of Passover, but it is true to God, for in His love, His passion, He shed His blood and allowed His body to be broken. He unites with us, as a man with His bride in His death, and we unite with Him when we are buried with Him in the baptism of His death and raised up in His resurrection. One of my favorite verses in the Song of Solomon 2:4, *He brought me to the banqueting house, and his banner over me was love.* This is the banqueting table, and His banner over us is love here.

You can have a heavy meal, but leanness of soul. You can eat all the good food of the world, take your body where you want to go, expose your mind to what you want, allow your purpose to go soft, and yet be hungry. You can gain the whole world but lose your soul. But this small meal will fill your soul. In fact, you couldn't fit on all the tables of the world, what God gives us by this table. The world can't buy this meal.

It is a table so lowly that anyone can reach it, yet so high and holy that no one can reach it without the Lord bringing it down to us, and no one can approach it without clean hands. Psalms 24: 3 - 4:

> ³Who shall ascend into the hill of the LORD? or who shall stand in his holy place? ⁴He that hath clean hands, and a pure heart; who hath not lifted up his soul unto vanity, nor sworn deceitfully.

So who can ascend the hill of the Lord—those who have been

cleansed by the blood.

John 6:37 (TMSG) "*37Every person the Father gives me eventually comes running to me. And once that person is with me, I hold on and don't let go.*" This was such an important meal, that God Himself had to prepare it, had to be it, had to hold it out to us, had to bring it low, had to make us able by grace to receive it, so we could be brought up high. The star of Christmas leads to this table. There was a bright shining star when Jesus was born, but the sun hid its face when He died. Yes, nature was in upheaval that day, the Son, Who was the instrument of creation had died. But I think another reason the sun hid its face was that a greater light shined extravagantly in the darkness—the Bright and Morning Star was shining on the cross. The greatest expression of love in the history of the world was there. Love is what shines bright. Love makes the world right. Love created us and love redeemed and recreated us. The purpose of this book is to mark you for God. I never want you to go back.

And as awesomely as God said, "Let there be light" at creation, He declares "Let there be light" at the cross, the kind of light that penetrates the darkness of this world. It is a light that surpasses the light of creation with the light of our re-creation and salvation.

God brought this table down to us. We could not reach it on our own. It is a meal so holy that no one can really partake of it with unclean hands and an unclean walk. So the word says, let us examine ourselves.

But we not only look God-ward in this table, we commune with each other, the body of believers, we break this bread with others. We share the body and blood, we are the body and we all have the blood. What can separate us from the love of God, the scripture says, but neither should we be separated from each other. We are dependent on God and each other. Let's not forget that. We are the body of Christ. We are Christ's physical expression in this earth and we have the great King as our God. If you are living a solitary life, Jesus invites you to join in the communion with Him and your brothers and sisters—you are not alone. If you are living without the communion that this table represents you are missing its purpose.

If you have a grudge against your brother or sister, best to leave it at the examining part and partake of the table with each other. You are missing it if you are judging your brother or sister. You are missing it if you are angry. You are missing it if you think in your heart, well they did so and so and I don't need them. Yes you need them. You need them because they help you learn how to love, and that is the most important lesson of all. Our natural instinct is to cut off people but God's supernatural instinct is to join people. Sometimes we think that we only need people who help us and are good to us. No, we need people we don't like, people that test our patience and ability to love. That is because those people stretch us, and help us to become more like Jesus. So thank God for those people, they are precisely the people God has sent to sit beside us. There are people that separate from the body of Christ, but perhaps they did not belong in the beginning, because belonging means just that, joined forever: 1 John 2:18 - 19:

> [18]Little children, it is the last time: and as ye have heard that antichrist shall come, even now are there many antichrists; whereby we know that it is the last time. [19]They went out from us, but they were not of us; for if they had been of us, they would *no doubt* have continued with us: but *they went out*, that they might be made manifest that they were not all of us.

Jesus didn't call us to like our neighbor but to love our neighbor, and that means, acting in accordance with the word of God in relation to the person next to you, your neighbor. Anyone can be good to someone who is good to them, though not always. The Lord did not tell us to like our neighbor as ourselves, but love them.

He also did not tell us to like the Lord our God, with all our heart mind and soul. He told us to love the Lord our God with all our heart mind and soul. And here is the problem of our modern culture. We like Him when He blesses us and makes us feel good, and want Him to give us a pass on our sins, but the cross is absolute. We like the Lord our God, but that is childish because He is calling us to take up our crosses and die daily. Do we like Him when He clearly shows us our behavior, attitudes and emotions, are against the word of God? That requires us to love the Lord our God. Do we like Him when He calls us to die, sacrifice, and obey? No, not always, but if we do, it shows we love Him. We can't pick and choose the scripture. He is God and we are not.

Let us now go to the table. 1 Corinthians 11:23 - 24:

> [23]For I have received of the Lord that which also I delivered unto you, That the Lord Jesus *the same* night in which he was betrayed took bread: [24]And when he had given thanks, he brake *it*, and said, Take, eat: this is my body, which is broken for you: this do in remembrance of me.

Jesus took the bread, He gave thanks and then He broke it. This too is the Biblical pattern. The breaking of the bread tells us of Jesus, our broken bread. Jesus, Who is to be devoured. His life is to be part of our system, going down to the blood and the spiritual DNA of our lives.

He takes His life, it is blessed and then broken. He offers Himself, He is blessed of the Father, what He offers is the food of God. He is broken and given to all. This is a picture of the cross, but also of the life that He gives freely to us. The breaking of the bread releases the anointing. We see here that the breaking of the bread brings revelation. The breaking of the bread brings nourishment. God intends also for us to be broken so His anointing and power can be released. Take eat, this is My body, which is broken for you, this do in remembrance of Me.

Next, we remember Jesus at the table. He tells us to do so. He says, remember Me as often as you take it. He says, remember Me as often as you take it. I have always loved the fact that Jesus asks to be remembered. We should be in holy awe of the sacrifice for this table. Look how vulnerable Jesus makes Himself here. Look He says, remember Me. God humbles Himself and asks for our love. Isn't that always the deepest cry of our hearts, see me, remember me, love me, see me. We all want to be loved because we were created in love, and God is love Who created us. But Jesus also says, I wanted your love and therefore I permitted myself to die in love for that love. God desires one thing, and that is our worship.

The price of our love was high. We love Him because He first loved us. As we come in holy awe, soberness of heart, and yet joy, we remember Him. Open your mouths and give the sacrifice of praise. 1 Corinthians 11:25:

> 25After the same manner also *he took* the cup, when he had supped, saying, This cup is the new testament in my blood: this do ye, as oft as ye drink *it*, in remembrance of me.

I could speak for weeks on the blood. It is the token of the new covenant. It can wash us as nothing on earth can wash us. I am so grateful for the blood of Jesus. He has washed my heart and continues to do so with His blood. It is powerful:

> 24You have come to Jesus, the one who mediates the new covenant between God and people, and to the sprinkled blood, which graciously forgives instead of crying out for vengeance as the blood of Abel did. Hebrews 12:24 (NLT).

Blood always cries out. When we are hurt the broken part of us cries out and when we hurt others their blood cries out, but the blood of Jesus cries out stronger and forgives, quenching the need for vengeance. A transfusion of eternal life is released at the cross through the blood, and by the living bread, His body, which He gives for the life of the world. The blood restores holiness, order—new DNA, ordered DNA, holy DNA, preservation of life on earth, and eternal life by closing the breaches and repairing the foundations of many generations caused by the destruction of sin. The blood is our red carpet to the throne room of God. Jesus is our holy Way. After Jesus rose again, He took that blood and placed it on the mercy seat in heaven, and so that blood always avails to wash away our sins.

26*For as often as ye eat this bread, and drink this cup, ye do show the Lord's death till he comes.* 1 Corinthians 11:26. Again, we celebrate the sacrifice of the cross until He comes. When He comes the day of the cross, the time of grace will be over. The time of salvation will be over. When He finally rules and reigns it is not going to be the last supper we will be taking, a remembrance of Him on earth, but the marriage supper of the Lamb, a joining with Him in heaven for an eternal celebration. We eternally rejoice because of the blood of Jesus, but we eternally celebrate because we are married to Him

Jesus wants His death remembered, over and over again. He made this simple supper so we would have no excuse. There is nothing elaborate that needs to be done, just a piece of bread and juice and the humbling of our hearts. He wants His death remembered, because we are in the time when His heart is open in love to the world, calling the world, to become worshippers. Remember Me, see how much I love you. Someday, when He comes, we will not be remembering Him. We will be in relationship with Him, or not.

[27]*Wherefore whosoever shall eat this bread, and drink this cup of the Lord, unworthily, shall be guilty of the body and blood of the Lord.* 1 Corinthians 11:27. Do not take this in an unworthy manner. The way we can take this in a worthy manner is truly to come and examine our hearts:

> [28]But let a man examine himself, and so let him eat of *that* bread, and drink of *that* cup. [29]For he that eateth and drinketh unworthily, eateth and drinketh damnation to himself, not discerning the Lord's body. 1 Corinthians 11:28 - 29.

We fail to discern the Lord's body when we irreverently come to this table, when we don't humble our hearts and speak truth to the Lord, and also when we don't discern our brothers and sisters in the body of Christ. We all belong to each other. So the results are felt:

> [30]For this cause many *are* weak and sickly among you, and many sleep. [31]For if we would judge ourselves, we should not be judged. [32]But when we are judged, we are chastened of the Lord, that we should not be condemned with the world. 1 Corinthians 11:30 - 32.

We can either judge ourselves at the cross or be judged by the cross. We have the opportunity here and every day to ask forgiveness, be cleansed, be made whole. When we judge ourselves it does not mean to be in criticism or self hatred of ourselves, but honestly look at our sins and faults and take them to the Lord—let them go, they are on His head. When we judge ourselves, we don't judge others. It says to judge yourself, not the person next to you. If we judge ourselves that we can come to the throne of grace, rather than be judged with the world at the great white throne judgment.

We have a great blessing, the power of the Holy Spirit working in us. It is the Spirit of Truth that can reveal the secrets of our hearts, why, to experience the cleansing, healing and strengthening of the blood. This is the heartbeat of God and the heart at the midst of the world. Come, come all ye that labor and are heavy laden, come to Jesus, He will not cast out anyone that comes to Him. Can't you feel God's heart here? It is a meal He prepared from the foundation of the world. It is His tokens of love.

I want to prepare you for communion always. Jesus was a Lamb prepared for us, but will you be a lamb for Him? He gave Himself willingly, will you give yourself willingly? Are we ready to surrender everything? The cross is a place of surrender, not war. The battle was finished there, all scores settled, all wars over.

The cross is a loving symbol, but it is also a frightening one—look what we did to our God. And we will die there, just as He died there, but He has taken the pain and the blows as He saves to the uttermost. All our eternal value is seen at the cross. I think we must realize that the tremendous love of the cross exists because of the awful judgment that needed to be taken for us. God so loved. God was driven to take the sins of the world because He knew the consequences. His love tells us of a heaven and a hell. It tells us of heaven, a new creation, and eternity in the love of God. The wages of sin is death, but the gift of God is eternal life. The word tells the sinner to forsake sin. It is not a popular message because the sins that beset us are the ones that trip us and take us back all the time. These are not the easy matters to take care of. They become part of our mind, emotions, body, lifestyle, finances. They are mixed into our being—we have been taken over by a spiritual killer. Yet

God calls for separation. It takes the power of the cross to do this. So today the question is, are you ready to go to the cross, and then take up your cross and follow Him? First we go to His cross, and then we take up our cross. It is the same question tomorrow and the next day and the day after that. Following Jesus is something worth living for and dying for. The cross is the great divide. On one side is communion where He takes our judgment and we die to self but live eternally, and on the other side is separation, where we live to ourselves, but take our judgment and die eternally. You and I are going to die no matter what, so we might as well die, following Jesus, rather than following ourselves or some other thing or person. You and I are going to live, no matter what, so we might as well live, following Jesus, rather than following ourselves or some other thing or person. The invitation is there—for now.

> [24]And when he had given thanks, he brake *it*, and said, Take, eat: this is my body, which is broken for you: this do in remembrance of me. [25]After the same manner also *he took* the cup, when he had supped, saying, This cup is the new testament in my blood: this do ye, as oft as ye drink *it*, in remembrance of me. 1 Corinthians 11:24 - 25.

CHAPTER TWENTY-ONE

Communion in Every Home
The Territory of the Cross

Take eat, this is My body which is broken for you, this do in remembrance of Me. This cup is the new testament in My blood; this do ye, as oft as ye drink it, in remembrance of Me. I Corinthians. 11:24 - 25.

He opens the door of His heart, and there He is miraculously, breaking bread that we may sup, and releasing His blood that we may wash our hearts from our sins.

Jesus is ready to enter every home. Behold He stands at the door and knocks that if any man should open up, He will come in and sup. Is the home ready? Will the true Master be allowed in? He waits as the true Bridegroom for His bride so that the marriage covenant might again be established and water be changed into wine.

God take the most ordinary and basic elements that belong to each home and each life, and makes them holy. Each house contains the elements of communion, the bread and the wine, waiting to be sanctified into a holy feast. Each person is flesh and blood, waiting to be energized by the Holy Spirit and molded into the image of Christ to do the will of the Father. Sleeping in ordinariness and isolation, the elements wait on shelves and cupboards for use by the master of the house, while unknown and unborn disciples dream in beds and cars of glory and power. One day the Master of the house changes, and the ordinary is suddenly transfigured and glorified. Bread and wine are set apart for the communion feast, and body and blood are merged with His body and blood on which the world may sup.

We all wait in our paths of ordinary life, waiting to be born into the glory of the sons and daughters of God; into that destiny for which we were born. We wait to be ignited with the light that "lighteth every man that entereth in the world," even before we recognize that light. This is the true light. We struggle to be seen, and some are, but that is not the triumph or the true light of which the gospel speaks. It is the path of the righteous man that is ordered of the Lord, so each step glows with His eternal dimension and glory. It is the fire shut up in our bones that must be carried to others to illuminate their lives with the Way, Truth, and Life of God.

Communion in every home. God chooses that which we all have: Body and blood, bread and wine. God chooses the material which all may offer to the feast, and through which all of His kingdom, power, and glory can be channeled from the Father above to the world. God chooses us, not the glory, but the ordinary. He wants us, so He can reproduce Him. He knows the value of the only creation that can be transformed into sons and daughters of God, and will not let it be lost at any cost.

To this end He lays a table before us, using the elements we have, Jesus broken like us, the small pieces and cups we all must drink, but which radiate life and covenant, so we may be resurrected like Him by the will of the Father through the power of the Holy Spirit. As He is, so are we in this world. Once transformed by the will of the Father, we may lay this table before others by the sacrifice of our lives, and therefore establish a continual feast through which the world may experience the life of God.

Bread and wine,

Body and blood,

Communion, reunion

God's tokens of love.

CHAPTER TWENTY-TWO

THE END, OR NOT

I am Alpha and Omega, the beginning and the
ending. Revelation. 1:8.

There is no end to a revelation of the cross, I can't stop writing
this book. It is the tree of life hidden in paradise and the door to
heaven with God. The cross is a story of glory without an ending,
not now, not until the final battles are won, the last resurrections, the
judgments rendered, the rewards given, the families reunited, the
curse finally broken, the tears wiped away, a new heaven and new
earth established, the kingdoms of this world become the kingdoms
of our God and of His Christ, the marriage supper of the Lamb, and
free access is given to the tree of life, so all that is left is eternal
worship and adoration of the One Who loved us and washed us from
our sins in His own blood. John writes:

> And there are so many other things which Jesus
> did, the which, if they should be written every one, I
> suppose that even the world itself could not contain
> the books that should be written. Amen. John 21:25.

So it is with the cross. The world itself could not contain the
books that could be written of what Jesus did at the cross. That
would be the whole history and revelation of salvation and re-
creation, for when Jesus said, "It is finished" and rested in death,
God's redemption, salvation, and re-creation of the human race was
completed.

Jesus promised us in John 14:12, "Verily, verily, I say unto you,

He that believeth on me, the works that I do shall he do also; and greater works than these shall he do; because I go unto my Father." However, can I propose the possibility that our idea of greater works may be somewhat different from the Father's? Our idea of greater works is big churches, huge crowds, miracles, supernatural events, healings, and millions of souls. After all, Jesus was sent to the lost sheep of the house of Israel, we are sent to the whole world. We would do greater works in His name—the scope would have to be bigger. And there is nothing wrong with that—He told us to go into all the world and preach the gospel to every living creature. He told us signs would follow those who believe. The world needs the preaching of the cross and the resurrection and the signs that follow.

But I think God's idea of "greater works" may be more in line with this, or perhaps, we should differentiate between "greater works" and "greatest work." God's greater works carry the weight of His glory in the dark. God's greater work was done by a solitary man, covered in blood, ripped to shreds, naked, bleeding His life out on a cross, abandoned by His Father, abandoned by all but one disciple, viewed in horror, compassion and trauma by His mother and a few women, breathing His last, between two thieves in front of a crowd of vicious spectators and brutal sadistic soldiers. God's greater work was stripped down to absolute love. Maybe that is God's idea of greater works. Remember that when you feel like a failure. Remember that in the dying times, the dark times, the weeping times. That was the greater work and the greatest work.

The cross is the lens through which we gaze on the glory of the crown, and through which eternal life is released in and to us by Jesus Christ. It is our access to know and dwell with God the Father, God the Son, and God the Holy Spirit, that He may know us and dwell in us. It is the instrument of healing and restoration and deliverance of the human race that God chooses. Rulership is only attainable in death and humility at the cross. It is our Mount of Transfiguration for the glory that lies before us, just as it was for Jesus. The transfiguration of our disfiguration is finished there. Through the cross we are *looking unto Jesus, the Author and Finisher of our faith, who for the joy that was set before Him endured the cross, despising the shame, and is set down at the right hand of the throne of God.* Hebrews 12:2. We become partakers of this same faith as we come to the cross, and then pick up our own crosses daily and die there.

The cross cuts "a-cross" over all national and political boundaries and geographical territories. It cancels race, gender, social and economic differences in this world, for it places us all under the rulership of God. By it dreams are sanctified, and hearts are purified. It travels into the past and present and future to cancel out the works of the enemy and cancel the multiplicity of our sins. Only the cross can break the terrible pull of flesh and blood, flesh which has its own desires, and blood that demands its own requirements. We all come from the same direction to the cross. It is the great equalizer. It erases all but the grace of God. It is the crossbars of a compass leading to heaven whereby our sins are removed as far as the east is from the west and our final destination is transformed as far as heaven is from hell.

At the cross we see the hands splintered with nails of pain, but the pain no longer exists. And so it is with our lives. That which brought ruin is separated from us forever by the cross. It is the great divine divide of all humanity. Either you have come to the foot of the cross or you have not.

Now is the time to come to the cross. Someday the straight and narrow gate will be closed because time will end. Instead of mercy there will be judgment on this earth for rejecting a second birth of love, and choosing instead a first birth of sorrow, clinging in pride to sin, self and differences. There will be a judgment that many long years ago was poured out on the sinless Son of God. Next, it will be poured out on sinful men and women who reject the merciful love of the Savior, and it will be a judgment poured on the earth itself, because all creation must be purified and judged whether willingly or unwillingly. It is His blood or ours.

Come to the cross. It is most alluring once you have tasted the sweet love of God there. He sanctifies our suffering at the cross, and we fellowship with His. We change through gratitude for this unspeakable gift, and learn to live and love again. There, as at the resurrection, and each intersection with our Lord, we worship at

His feet. Death loses its sting and the grave loses its victory there. Death and the grave have no power over those who have already experienced death and the grave. The sting of death is sin. Sin dies and death dies. The grave dies, and time dies. These are swallowed up in victory by eternal life. When we surrender at the cross, we gain the Person, position, purpose, promises, and power of the cross. That is the great exchange. It is the open door to the divine destiny in the dimension desired for each one of us. In Revelation 3:20, Jesus says, "Behold, I stand at the door and knock, and if any man will hear My voice and open the door, I will come in to him and sup with him and he with Me." Jesus is knocking. Hear His voice. Open the door. Do not make the Savior wait. Come. Take the bread and the cup, and sup.

THE END FOR NOW

We hope you enjoyed *A Revelation of the Cross* and that you found it a blessing. If you desire to enter communion with the Father, Son and Holy Spirit, pray this simple prayer: "Dear Heavenly Father, I ask Jesus into my heart as my Lord and Savior. I know I am a sinner, but I believe that the blood of Jesus cleanses me from all sin. I repent of my sins and give my life to Jesus Christ, receiving His life in return. Fill me with Your Holy Spirit. In Jesus' name. Amen."

For similar uplifting books from Signalman Publishing, please visit our website at www.signalmanpublishing.com.

SIGNALMAN
PUBLISHING

www.ingramcontent.com/pod-product-compliance
Lightning Source LLC
LaVergne TN
LVHW051235080426
835513LV00016B/1596